YOU DECIDE
WHAT 'C' STANDS FOR

FOR

A Daughter's Legacy For Her Mum

By

Sarah Davies

This book is dedicated to My Mum

The very bravest person I have known

My inspiration

For making me believe hope is underrated

For helping me see the power of the mind is
undervalued

For being my best friend

All the brave women and their families

battling this horrific fight.

CONTENTS

ACKNOWLEDGMENTS

Special thanks to …

My husband Simon. With me every step of the way, no judgements just unconditional love.

My children Sam, Scarlett, and Pippa. For checking how I was feeling constantly and giving me love and humour (including Lauren).

My brother Dave and sister Sian and their families Veronica, Martha, Lyla, Luke, and Megan who were going through their own individual hell.

My aunties Lauren and Vel and uncles Clive and Si for knowing when to step in and help when I was on the edge.

My in-laws Ian, Lin, Kerry, and Wayne for being ever supportive.

My best friends for never getting bored of me, for allowing me to rant, offering lots of tissues and lots and lots of gin (especially Lol and Minty).

Mum's best friend Tony who did everything he could to help in the dark days.

My work friends for making work a safe sanctuary

for me and for supplying my Mum with chip sticks (thank you Stan).

Dr H for giving Mum hope and never giving up on her.

My favourite bands, The View, Courteeners, Liam Gallagher, Kyle Falconer, Gerry Cinnamon, stereophonics, and Reverend and the makers for giving me their music to light the way throughout this journey.

Allie from *Flowers by Allie* for her beautiful and genius flowers.

Please note this voyage has some bad language in it. I tried to keep the dialect restrained but as it unfolds, I hope you can understand. It is not meant in any way to offend.

Written at her Mum's bedside during various treatments, join a daughter's experience of her Mum's ovarian 'C' journey.

The highs, the lows, the bright, the funny, and the dark, sad times. This aims to help raise awareness of one of the 'silent' killers.

"Within the darkest, dark moments there are twinklings of extreme brightness."

In aid of

ovarian cancer

10% of each book sale to be donated.

THE INTRODUCTION

This is the story of my Mum's journey with that bastard that is known as cancer, ca, the BIG C. I don't have to spell out what the 'C' stands for. Anyone who has had their world plummet to the depths of despair when the doctor utters those simple but all-consuming words "I'm sorry but you have cancer" will have their own version and thoughts as to what that 'C' actually stands for.

I'm not actually sure why I'm writing this and I'm certainly not sure if anyone will read and be interested. My story is no more special or hard-hitting than anyone else's. I'm hopeful it will be cathartic for me and of some support to anyone who travels this lonely quest. I'd also like to think that it may help to. raise awareness of this truly devastating disease that works quietly before dragging its victim into the depths of its shadows.

I feel it is crucial initially to explain my family situation:

My Dad died suddenly in 2002. Mum often said Dad wouldn't have been able to deal with her illness, it would have destroyed him.

I have an older sister, Sian, who unfortunately lived in Dubai when Mum was travelling on this horror ride. My younger brother, Dave, lived in London with a young family and an incredibly supportive wife Veronica, but like I said they lived in London, over 250 miles from Mum.

The distance between my siblings and I was as frustrating for them as it was for me. I lived a 40 minutes' drive from my Mum, so near yet on occasions felt so far.

Me, I had an excellent support network. My husband of forever, three children who all did everything they could to make things easier, and good, good friends always ready to lend an ear or a glass of gin.

Unfortunately, I was a registered nurse of 20 odd years, I will explain the 'unfortunately' part at a later point.

I'd like to give some details of Mum to encourage connection, after all she is the leading lady in this. It's hard to condense 'Mum' into a few sentences to do her the justice she deserves but I just want to give you a quick overview.

Mum and Dad had such an obvious and deep love for each other, I can honestly hand on heart say I never heard them argue. In later years I actually asked her if they ever in fact did. "Of course, we had disagreements, we just didn't want to do it in front of you kids," she replied. These family values were important to them.

I also found out in later years they had got engaged after two weeks of meeting, at the age of 18. This was a fact never revealed until we were all older, probably in case we followed suit.

I always imagined my Mum and Dad would grow old together, sitting on a bench eating chocolate, although I'm sure those who knew them well could see a bottle of red wine instead! This wasn't meant to be though. Dark days were upon us when in 2002 Dad died suddenly, aged 55. Mum never completely got over this but took to travelling to escape reality. Mum loved to explore other countries; she would take off on her own. This was something I always admired about her. Her gusto and daring nature were always unwavering. During her travels many a 'Jan moment' occurred.

She rang me distressed from Thailand on one occasion. Her tour guide had offered to show her a restaurant for lunch. He proceeded to follow her in, sit her down, and started spoon-feeding her whilst telling her his wife didn't understand him. Mum excused herself for the toilet and did a runner out of the back door!

Whilst in Australia Mum had hotel problems so ended up having to stay in a backpacker's hostel. She ended up paying for the whole dormitory as she didn't want to share with young, lively backpackers.

Mum came back from one Indian trip with her nose pierced as she felt like just rebelling.

Mum certainly was a character. She loved to chat a lot, had a wicked sense of humour, she was very friendly, loyal, and loved her family and friends fiercely.

Mum was a force to be reckoned with on her sewing machine, a talent I sadly didn't inherit, in fact, none of us did. When I say Mum was good, it was on a scale that she made mine and my sister's wedding dresses; we rated her so highly when she offered there was no hesitation and an absolute honour to have her do this.

Mum was an intelligent soul; she had the mind of an encyclopaedia and a photographic memory, Mum never forgot.

She was the sort of person that could comfortably engage with random strangers and think nothing of it. She was also the sort of person that would always have a peek in a pram and cooo at any baby, every baby.

Mum had spirit and a good soul. She was loyal and loving and, as I found out, brave, so very, very brave. She was the bravest person I have known.

4

My Mum was not only the bravest person I have known but the most determined too. In the face of adversity, she confronted things face on. You could almost see her gritting her teeth as she took on various challenges sent her way. When Dad was alive, she would never drive as it frightened her (she had passed her test years previously). Once she lost him, she had a couple of refresher lessons and just got on with it. Mum being Mum wasn't happy to just potter around locally in her car, no not her, she would drive hundreds of miles from one side of the country to the other to visit her parents regularly, hating every minute of the drive, I should add. This is just one example of her typical pure determination.

Mum was immensely proud of her grandchildren: Luke, Megan, Sam, Scarlett, Pippa, Martha, and Lyla. They all lit up her life in different ways, she loved any time spent with any of them, as they did too. She had extraordinarily strong bonds with them all and would do anything for any of them. The older grandchildren – Luke, Meg, and Sam – were one of the things that got her through Dad's death.

Mum loved her 'in-laws', referring to Simon (my husband) and Veronica (my brother's wife) as her son and daughter. They both in turn loved her back.

Mum had strong opinions, some I shared, some I didn't. We would often have to agree to disagree and had many a lively debate.

Mum was very much a stay-at-home Mum during our earlier years. She was lucky enough to be able to do this, and we were lucky too. If we'd had a bad day, she'd be there to greet us with hugs and kind words. Baking was another of Mum's talents, quite often we would get home to the aroma of cakes or biscuits. Days off from school due to sickness often consisted of being tucked up on the sofa watching soaps with Mum whilst she sat on the floor surrounded by her latest sewing project. We all loved this time in our lives. We really had the perfect childhood; one everyone strives to give their own children. One every child wished they had.

Our 'C' journey as a family began in the Autumn of 2014. Before I begin it is important to understand there had been no previous history of 'C' in our family. This was incomprehensible. This 'thing' can catapult you with no warning and absorb you whole.

THE BEGINNING

Mum rang me on a random morning, she had been to see her GP as the previous night she had been extremely restless due to tummy ache. Her doctor guessed irritable bowel syndrome but took a full set of bloods to rule out anything more sinister, thankfully. Mum, convinced she had IBS, asked me if I knew what she should be eating, I advised her maybe the 40 dates and figs she ate each evening would be better off abandoned. We laughed. Mum was bright, she assured me she had no other symptoms and felt fine. She had climbed to the top of Mount Snowdon a couple of months prior to this night, a task anyone who knew her would find highly amusing. Mum was not a hiker; in fact, she was not a walker and would rather drive even the shortest of distances. She did it to keep a friend company, begrudgingly I might add! All joking aside, this demonstrates just how 'fine' Mum was until that bolt out of the blue struck. This demonstrates why we should not ignore even relatively minor symptoms; it demonstrates how sneaky 'C' can be, it can work quietly before announcing "BAM here I am" at the top of its voice! 'C' is a cheater, a wretch, and a destroyer of normality, creating a new kind of normal. I do feel now Mum may admit that she hadn't felt 'quite' right for a while but put it down to 'innocent' changes in her body and felt she could justify them all … I mean, 'C' nah, no way!

A few days later, Mum rang me in a panic. Her GP had advised her she needed an urgent ultrasound as some of her blood results were abnormal, in particular her ovarian markers. (The blood test carried out is called a CA125 test. If the levels are raised, it's not an automatic indicator of ovarian 'C'. It can be indicative of less sinister conditions such as: endometriosis, menstruation, ovarian cysts. An ultrasound scan has to be carried out of the abdomen and pelvis. This will allow a GP to gain a fuller picture.) This in turn sent me into a panic. For some reason ovarian 'C' has always been the one health condition that had terrified me. But … come on, no history of any 'C' in our family, let alone ovarian, Mum climbed Snowdon recently, she had only had one night of tummy ache. I assured Mum that it was probably just precautionary, and all would be fine. I believed this at that time.

The ultrasound, however, was the bearer of the

news we'd been dreading. 'C' was a definite possibility.

One of the hardest things I found to deal with, especially initially, was the time it took to have answers. In one respect it happened too quickly, but in another, diagnosis seemed to take forever. There was some confusion as to where the 'C' was. The gynaecologist (a Doctor specialising in the health of the female reproductive system – vagina, uterus, and ovaries) said it definitely wasn't ovarian, the gastroenterologist (a Doctor specialising in the health of the digestive system) said it definitely wasn't bowel related and around and around we'd go. I became very mindful of time. The longer it took to decide where the bastard was lurking the longer the wait to start the fight to eradicate it. Finally, it was decided it was defiantly ovarian of origin. OK so we now knew what we were dealing with. Well, partly! Mum didn't want to know any specific details; hence we didn't really know any details. We were unsure of stage/grade and therefore prognosis. I understood both sides. Mum said if she knew the whole story, she'd lose hope and maybe even her will to live, for me it was difficult as I was to be Mum's main carer and I was unsure of the practicalities that lay ahead. Ultimately it was Mum's disease so we would deal with it however she wanted to and be guided by her needs. This was her journey and we were only along for the ride; Mum was the navigator.

Let's discuss some cold, hard facts surrounding ovarian 'C':

Every year 7,300 women in the UK are diagnosed with ovarian 'C'. Almost 6 in 10 women are diagnosed at a late stage in England (2014). Frightening? Yep! Better news, however, is that almost half of all women diagnosed with ovarian 'C' survive their disease for five years or more (2010-11). Ovarian 'C' is 'C' arising from the cells in and around the ovary and fallopian tubes. There are many different types of ovarian tumours classified by the types of cells and tissue they originate from.

I feel it is also imperative to mention those pesky, maybe not so innocent symptoms that should be addressed rather than brushed to one side. Know what is normal for your body. It is better to pop along to your GP and get them checked out … it is always better to be safe than sorry, that visit could save your life.

Persistent bloating

Feeling full quickly and/or experiencing loss of appetite

Pelvic or abdominal pain

Urinary symptoms (urgency or frequency)

Occasionally there can be other symptoms:

Changes in bowel habit (diarrhoea or constipation)

Extreme fatigue (feeling very tired)

Unexplained weight loss

Any bleeding after the menopause should always be investigated by a GP.

Symptoms will be:

Frequent – they usually rear their bastard heads more than 12 times a month

Persistent – they don't bugger off

New – they are alien for you

I went through a period where I was convinced I had ovarian 'C' – I had persistent pelvic pain lasting a few weeks. I was absolutely terrified, I won't lie. I became unreasonably paranoid to be honest. My GP was extremely understanding and sent me for an urgent internal ultrasound. I was lucky, my results confirmed a fibroid. That gave me a tiny insight of how terrifying the whole ordeal must be.

To make matters worse for my Mum, as if this was possible, the week before she was firmly diagnosed with the chain around the neck, her 'C', her Mum, my Nan, died. This was devastating for Mum as although Nan was old, they were remarkably close. I'm not sure Mum ever had the chance to truly grieve as she had to quickly change into combat mode to fight the fight of her life, for her life. The day Mum was told

Nan only had two weeks to live, she was at an appointment with the gastroenterologist at the same hospital Nan was in. This was when the doctors weren't sure still if Mum's 'C' was bowel or ovarian related. We had the call to get to Nan's ward as the doctor wanted to talk to her, to give her this news. Can you imagine that?

In the midst of all the devastation my eldest, my son, left to embark on his adventure that is University. He had chosen to go to Sheffield, which was great, but it was over 150 miles from home. This was a massive change to our family dynamics.

So, we now knew origin, not prognosis, and the next step was into the place Mum said always made her full of fear. The 'C' specialist hospital. This was an hours' drive usually through rush hour and parking was always a real struggle. This baffled me as people entering were obviously stressed without trying to find somewhere to leave their vehicle. To be honest it didn't just baffle me, it irritated the absolute hell out of me, not how you want to feel whilst trying to put your passenger at ease. If you're like me you find it hard to disguise your utter annoyance, I tried though, I really did.

I always had mixed feelings about the 'C' hospital. On one hand it was a beacon of hope but at the same time it was sad, just sad. On one hand it felt safe like a bubble, but at the same time it felt an air of desperation.

Like I said, mixed, conflicting feelings indeed.

Another thing I couldn't get my head around was the waiting times to see Mum's oncologist, we would have to wait on average 90 minutes over appointment time. I'm not even exaggerating. That was a long, long wait for people so ill and quite often terrified. To be fair though once Mum finally had her name called out and entered the oncologist's room there was no rushing. She was given undivided attention for as long as she needed. Mum and I used to play a game whilst waiting at her latter visits. Spot the wig, we used to enjoy guessing who had wigs and who had their own hair, it was never obvious. Wigs have come a long way! It sounds tasteless writing it, but it was harmless fun and Mum had her own wig by then. I'm sure we weren't the only ones playing either. If you've spent time somewhere similar, I'm sure you'll understand. If possible, where possible inject humour. That saying you either laugh or cry rings true. Mum was a laugher, this proved both positive and challenging for me, from a purely selfish perspective, I will elaborate later.

The 'C' hospital had a band of jolly, truly kind volunteers. There was a little gift shop that sold lots of trinkets and cards and always provided a warm welcome. Mum and I would often have a nose in there to while away the long wait for her name call. A small takeaway café was situated at the back of the waiting area. Mum would have a cup of tea and crisps

(I'm sure she had an addiction to crisps), I would have a diet coke and a bag of those yoghurt-covered raisins you can get. I convinced myself they were the healthy option.

Mum's oncologist I shall refer to as Dr H. A lovely, smiley, small lady whose bedside manner was exemplary. Mum had the greatest faith in her, she gave Mum hope. To Mum she was almost superhuman. Her life was in Dr H's hands. Meeting Dr H was the first time my being a nurse proved unfortunate. Mum was so enormously proud of this and took great delight in telling every doctor and nurse we met. The problem was as I kept telling them all oncology was not my speciality and it was all alien to me., also this involved my Mum, we were on the other side of the fence. The other problem I encountered throughout the whole journey was the case of 'knowing too much but not enough' I would spend hours researching and would put my own take on the results, sometimes reading the wrong things into everything, twisting them to fit whatever frame of mind I happened to have in that instance. I spent hours and hours researching, searching for answers. Mum, I don't think, ever did. She always said what she didn't know couldn't hurt her. Mum seemed far more at peace than I ever was. I, on the other hand, became completely paranoid. Cross at those who'd be positive and say all would be OK, cross at those who'd be negative and would say all would not be OK. It really was a no-win situation for others, I must have been hard to deal with, I can see that. Perhaps that highlighted a point, too much information is not necessarily a positive concept.

Mum had a great sense of faith; this she found a massive comfort throughout. She went to Church regularly but wasn't overly religious. She grasped at anything and everything that she felt could help her triumph. Reiki became a favourite (reiki: a mending technique based on the principle that a therapist can channel **energy** into the individual by means of touch, to activate the natural **healing** processes of the individual's body and restore physical and emotional well-being). Another therapy Mum immersed herself in was crystal healing. This she had carried out face to face, but also through distance healing. (Crystal healing is an alternative medical technique in which crystals and other stones are used to cure ailments and protect against disease. Proponents of this technique believe that crystals act as conduits for healing – allowing positive, healing energy to flow into the body as negative, disease-causing energy flows out.) Mum was willing to try anything. She surrounded herself with crystals, we'd tease her about this.

Mum's treatment plan was agreed: three cycles of chemotherapy, three weeks apart, CT scan to see effectiveness of the chemo, full hysterectomy, and removal of ovaries, three more cycles of chemotherapy. Job done! Hmmm sounds so easy!

The word chemotherapy derives from two words – chemical and therapy. It is a drug treatment given to destroy 'C' cells, unfortunately its navigational skills aren't perfect, and it obliterates any healthy cells within its path too. Its main problem is the inability to differentiate between 'C' cells and normal cells.

Prior to Mum's first chemotherapy dose we attended a chemo information session. This was helpful and informative. I would recommend anyone offered to attend. It takes the fear of the unknown out of the world of chemotherapy slightly. The one bit of information Mum homed in on was the suggestion to have some false nails sorted prior to the chemo as it can make your nails dark and cracked. Mum became obsessed with her nails following this and throughout her whole trek. Her nails always looked immaculate; this was important to her. It did cause problems on occasions though as the oxygen saturation machine struggled to get a proper reading and Mum's toes often had to be used as plan B.

Mum was given a voucher for a free wig before her chemo cycles begun. She had decided she didn't want to wear a head scarf as she didn't feel confident enough and felt personally it would highlight her illness to others. I found the day we went to choose a wig more difficult than Mum did. The staff were extremely sensitive and astute. They could sense I was struggling and kindly took me to a different room where the tears flowed. Mum choose her wig, she joked about getting a multi coloured wig to 'shock' everyone. She ended up getting one that ... well, looked exactly like her own hair! So much for shock tactics I joked. Mum looked at ease and confident in her new hair accessory. She had a look of determination that stated, 'bring this battle on!'

As well as offering the clinical assistance, Mum's 'C' hospital were incredibly supportive in organising benefits she was entitled to. Mum became entitled to a blue disabled parking badge and attendance allowance. This benefit was to enable payment of any personal care, cleaning, shopping, or domestic services payed for. It was paid directly to Mum every week. The staff at the 'C' hospital completed all the supporting documents for Mum as they were a bit tricky for her to focus on, feeling so unwell.

Mum's chemo sessions tended to be on a Friday. We had to go to the 'C' hospital on the Tuesday before to ensure all bloods were satisfactory to proceed.

Something Mum found valuable, and I would recommend to anyone about to undergo chemotherapy sessions, is a chemo kit. Mum's chemo kit comprised of:

- Blanket – for comfort and warmth as Mum had long sessions
- Travel pillow – again for comfort and extra support
- iPad and headphones – with films/ programmes downloaded for entertainment
- Snacks
- Drinks
- Ginger sweets – for anti-sickness properties
- Lavender pillow spray – for relaxation properties
- Hand heat warmers

As Mum's treatment progressed her veins were more difficult to locate, making cannulation particularly challenging and very painful. I used to cringe for Mum as staff tried for success. We discovered that heat warmers on the outside of hands popped in gloves a couple of hours prior to chemo gave a good result. These allowed for easier cannulation. When the body is warm, blood flow increases, dilating the veins and making them easier to find. These little handwarmers were a game changer for Mum.

Mum's chemo regime consisted of two drugs: Taxol and carboplatin. We arrived at the chemotherapy unit at 8.30 a.m. and left at 5 p.m. We were first in and last out. Patients came and went all day, we didn't! The first session was intimidating as we didn't know what to expect. I'm not sure what I had imagined but imagination can be worse than reality. The staff were warm, kind, and welcoming. They escorted Mum to a comfortable, reclining chair, I sat on a chair beside her. Mum was given the option of a 'cold cap' to wear during treatment. This had to be worn at each chemo treatment for the entirety and small amounts of time before and after. The idea of this was to reduce hair loss. It worked by decreasing the blood flow to the scalp, therefore lowering the amount of chemotherapy medication reaching that area. Mum declined as she said she was more worried about her nails than her hair! An initial IV drip was set up as a flush (the flush clears any blood or medicine from inside the IV line, so the line won't get blocked. This keeps the entry area clean and sterile. The procedure reduces the risk of infection and clogging, which can block important blood vessels and cause such problems as tissue damage). Then Mum had anti-sickness and antihistamine infusion before the big boys. The day went quickly, Mum was given many refreshments and we chatted to other patients and their chemo buddies. Mum managed to sleep for some time, it was nice to see her so relaxed. Finally, it was over, and I was able to take Mum back to my house to recover. I kept a chemo diary, as this was recommended to keep track and compare each chemo session as side effects tended to run in the same pattern for each dose given. However, this wasn't to be for Mum as we would soon find out.

Mum's biggest fear before commencing her chemotherapy was sickness, an affliction I'm sure many of us could relate to. During the chemo session, all 'newbies' were advised there was no reason to fear this as so many drugs were given to counteract this blight of a side effect. Chemo is renowned for making its victims very, very sick, isn't it? We were dubious about this affirmation but hopeful. I have to say, hand on heart, nausea and vomiting were successfully kept at bay throughout Mum's initial chemo cycles. We were yet to realise this, however, would be the least of Mum's problems.

Day 1 – absolutely fine, very good diet, very bright. Spent all day downstairs chatting non-stop! This is a breeze!

Day 2 – great day, no pain, no sickness, very good diet – in fact eating non-stop (must be the steroids)!

Day 3 – niggly constipation, no sickness, good diet, happy and still chatty in mood

Day 4 – some discomfort, fair diet, no sickness (thank goodness), continues to chat and enjoy conversation.

Day 5 – poorly, constipated, vomiting, taste changes, in bed all day

Day 6 – hospital!!

This is as far as the chemo diary went, the next steps in Mum's story made it get put on the back burner.

One of the things Mum was given before her chemotherapy commenced was a helpline card. This little card was to become my go-to reference, my little bible. This included her NHS number, 'C' hospital number, types of chemo invading her body, and a list of reasons to contact the helpline. These were as follows:

- A temperature above 37.5 C on two occasions 30 minutes apart, or one reading of 38.0 C
- A temperature below 35.5 C
- Feeling shivery or shaky
- Flu-like symptoms, chesty cough, or any other signs of infection
- Unusual bruising, bleeding, or rashes
- More than four episodes of diarrhoea in a 24-hour period or a stomach bug
- A sore mouth or mouth ulcers that prevents eating or drinking

Mum didn't like having her temperature checked daily, maybe it was because it was a constant reminder of the vulnerability of her body, I think she was absolutely terrified of the result, each time.

It's very hard following the first chemo session to tell what is and what isn't a problem. Were these things normal? I would say gut feeling had a lot to do with my response. I didn't feel like a nurse during this scenario, but I imagine it must've helped. I rang the helpline who advised me to take Mum to the A & E nearest to my home. They told me Mum probably just needed an enema, regular laxatives prescribed, and would then be on her way. If only, if only!

We arrived at A & E and were taken straight into a separate cubical, the hospital took the risk of neutropenia-related sepsis very seriously (neutropenia is the presence of abnormally few neutrophils in the blood, leading to increased susceptibility to infection). Another sly little bastard individual's undergoing chemo must be vigilant about.

What happened next was all a bit of a whirlwind but to cut a long story short, following numerous tests and scans, it was declared that Mum had a bowel obstruction. Her ovarian tumour had taken over and blocked her bowel. This was serious. The doctors spoke honestly and told me they weren't sure Mum would survive. They discussed the options, or should I say option. One option: bowel surgery, remove the damaged bowel and form an ileostomy if they were successful. An ileostomy is where the small bowel (small intestine) is diverted through an opening in the tummy (abdomen). This would result in a stoma bag (to collect waste products). This was shit! Literally!! The doctors were completely transparent and advised me if they were unable to perform an ileostomy it would be a case of making Mum comfortable for the extremely limited time she would have left. They didn't rate her chances; it was that bad. It all occurred on what would have been my Dad's Birthday if he had still been alive. I convinced myself that he was now Mum's Guardian Angel and there was no way he would let anything happen to her. Let's not forget my Nan, Mum's Mum, had not long died. I took some comfort in the fact that maybe the pair of them together, Dad and Nan, would block those pearly gates. Surely, they weren't ready to take Mum from us quite yet?

Mum, luckily for her, was high on the drugs she'd had pumped all day and seemed at peace with the unfolding quagmire. Me, I felt an overwhelming sense of complete and utter panic. Of course, I couldn't allow that to be apparent. Mum always had this habit of really studying my face intently for signs of worry or stress. She would always gauge her progress by my expressions and my eyes she said were always a dead giveaway! No pressure then! By now thankfully I had mastered my poker face. It was at that point that Mum made me sit on the end of her bed and take notes on her funeral wishes. She went into great depth, including where she would like her ashes, what songs, hymns etc. that were important to her. She also made me write down who she wanted to have miscellaneous possessions of hers when she had died. I had to promise I would carry out all her wishes. Can you imagine how difficult it was to be having that conversation without showing any emotion!? Words cannot describe the difficulty it posed to me, an emotional wreck by then. Mum hand wrote a little letter for my brother, sister, and me.

Within half an hour of rambling phone calls my support network had descended. This consisted of my husband, my best friend Lol, and my Aunties and Uncles (Mum's brothers and their wives). By now Mum had gone down to have her surgery, obliviously happy and high on her medications. We spent our time waiting for the surgery to be over at a nearby restaurant. Needless to say, none of us ate anything. The time dragged and dragged and dragged. The nurses on the ward had promised to ring as soon as they heard anything from theatre, this didn't stop me from ringing them again and again and again. Finally, they rang to let me know Mum was in recovery. They didn't have any details, just that she had survived the surgery. We got back to the hospital where my husband and I made our way up to the ward. The others stayed downstairs in reception to await news of Mum's fate. We had told them if it was the news we had prayed for we would come back down with our thumbs up. On our climb upstairs we could hear a voice calling to us. It was Mum! She was being wheeled on her trolley back to her ward. She looked so happy. She said she had checked and had a stoma bag in situ. She kept asking if we were happy. Mum could never imagine how ecstatic we were in that moment of time. We walked back to her ward with her, then run down to reception with the biggest grins and thumbs up. That was a triumph, that was one of the 'fuck you' 'C' occasions. My Mum, her body and mind were machines I then decided.

We all left Mum that night at the hospital, intoxicated on life and medications in the capable hands of the surgical team, the relief was immense, but the worry was no easier. It was hard to be completely at ease as Mum still had a very lengthy trudge through unchartered waters and uneven terrain to complete. Bowel obstruction was something we hadn't given any thought to, so it was a massive shock. After reading more about ovarian 'C' it isn't that uncommon and certainly something women need to be aware of following diagnosis. In hindsight I would've acted quicker to raise concerns had I known.

Recovery from surgery was slow but steady for Mum. She spent days attached to every machine possible (well, it looked like that at the time). Mum's mindset remained positive and light-hearted. By now she had named her stoma, calling it 'Gloria'. Gloria was a lady she knew from her past and had little regard for. Mum delighted in telling all the doctors and nurses the reason for the name … "it's an old bag and full of shit" she'd laugh. Mum embraced life initially with 'Gloria'; it had saved her life.

There were a couple of 'hairy' moments visiting Mum throughout her stay. On one occasion, I went into her room to find Mum surrounded by seven doctors. They explained that Mum's oxygen levels were worrying low, by this time she was having two litres of oxygen. They discussed the possibility of taking her into ITU and intubating her (intubation is the process of inserting a tube, called an endotracheal tube (ET), through the mouth and then into the airway. This is done so that a patient can be placed on a ventilator to assist with breathing during anaesthesia, sedation, or severe illness). They advised me that she might not make it out of there. However, as quickly as her oxygen levels had plummeted they had just as quickly risen again! I'm not sure how or why or what had happened, to be truthful I'm not sure the Doctors knew either, but Mum was back on track.

Another moment was when Mum was given tramadol post-operatively. This didn't agree with her.

She said it made her feel like she was dying, hence that was regarded an unsuitable medication for her moving forward. No one dared give it to her, her reaction had been both frightening and extreme.

The staff were kind and considerate. Mum forged good relationships with many of them, partly since she was a moderate stayer (anything between 5–21 days), partly because she was so very poorly. They were very communicative, which I appreciated and found sometimes this was a downside to the care given in other hospitals Mum visited. On one occasion, a nurse rang me to tell me that she had had to shave Mum's hair and she wanted me to have warning before I visited. Mum was at the stage of her chemo that hair started to come out. Even though it's a well-known side effect, it's one of those things you don't believe until it actually happens. Initially it's a few strays here and there, becoming more and more over the following days. It's then that many women make the decision to shave it before it gets too 'wispy'; that was the decision Mum made. Mum told me when I visited later that day that the nurse who'd shaved her hair, a newly qualified nurse, had cried silently whilst she'd shaved Mum's hair. Mum could feel the nurse's teardrops on her bare scalp.

The rest of Mum's stay went relatively smoothly, it lasted 18 days. Her blood results were unstable on occasions, leading to blood transfusions ('C' patients may need blood to compensate for one of the side effects of the chemotherapy drugs they receive. Chemotherapy drugs affect fast-dividing normal cells as well as the 'C' cells. The drugs can't differentiate between the good and bad cells. Bone marrow, which is like a factory for blood cell production, is also affected by chemotherapy due to its fast dividing cells. As a consequence, 'C' patients receiving chemotherapy treatment have decreased ability to produce new blood cells and are not able to replace blood cells that have been destroyed. This leads to patients' blood cell counts dropping and so transfusion of red cells and or platelets may be needed. Blood transfusions help manage symptoms patients experience due to low blood cell counts and enable them to continue their 'C' treatments) and Mum also required magnesium infusions ('C' patients may need magnesium to compensate for a side effect of the chemotherapy drugs they receive. Chemotherapy can affect renal function leading to a drop in magnesium blood levels. It can also cause chronic diarrhoea which can lead to a depleted level of magnesium). Mum took all of this in her stride, her only focus was to get well enough to get out and on with the battle in hand.

At home, back at mine, rehabilitation following hospital was comparatively peaceful. The only real flaw was an infection in Mum's wound, this was sorted promptly with oral antibiotics.

Mum was rightfully apprehensive leading up to her next chemo session. We all were. Her chemo had been put back three weeks to ensure her body and mind had time to recover from the major surgery she had endured, the pre chemo check-up went smoothly and it was blast off again a few days later!

This time the days between chemo cycles were uneventful. Mum managed to spend a short time at her home on her own. She had this crazy idea that she needed her kitchen and bathrooms completely gutted and 'redone'; in her mind it was the best time as she was spending so much time convalescing at mine. As I said I just thought it was a crazy idea. But 'redone' her kitchen and bathrooms were, and a messy process it was at that!

Following Mum's third chemo cycle she had to have a CT scan. This was to ascertain whether the chemo was actually doing its job of smashing the 'C' cells out of the park. My brother, sister, and I waited uneasily with Mum at the 'C' hospital waiting for the dreaded results. As always, the clinic was running well behind. These situations really were a slow form of torture. Mum sat humming, she did this when she was terrified, she told me later. This was really my only way of knowing how she truly felt as she put such a brave face on and was never quite honest about her feelings. We were all trying to be positive, but at the same time all expecting the worst.

Mum's name was finally announced. It was a tough walk to Dr H's room. We had to prop each other up. There was an overwhelming sense of terror that I know we all felt. It hung heavily in the air.

Dr H kindly cut to the chase as if sensing our fear. She took great pleasure in declaring Mum's 'C' was responding significantly well to the army of chemo sent in to fight the bastard 'C' cells. It was actually working! Relief doesn't cover it. For the first time then, since the beginning, I thought Mum may have a chance of winning her battle. Mum had won the first war. We got used to taking each day at a time during this campaign, every little victory brought immense joy at that point of time. It was a happy car ride back to Mum's. We had lunch on the way to celebrate the news. It was a contradictory journey from the one we'd had just three hours previously. Mum enjoyed ringing around to spread the great news to all. It was a good day.

Mum's next stride was to have a full hysterectomy. She was offered a bilateral oophorectomy; the surgeon advised her the choice was hers. Mum decided she wanted to get rid of as much as was possible. I swear she'd have had all of her internal organs removed if possible. "I want to reduce the chance of any stray sods hiding," she said. This was to be her second major surgery within four months. (A hysterectomy is a surgical procedure to remove the womb (uterus). A bilateral oophorectomy is the surgical procedure to remove both ovaries.)

The day of the operation was another one full of trepidation. Call me pessimistic but for some reason I expected the surgeon to open Mum up and close her straight away. You have to remember we did not know Mum's prognosis. We had no idea how far this evil curse had spread. Sometimes ignorance is bliss, others it leaves your mind open to all scenarios. I had visions of the surgeon telling us Mum was 'riddled', I had gained a small amount of information following Mum's discharge following her bowel obstruction surgery. I knew the 'C' had metastasised to her bowel, but beyond that, I had no idea. Again, it was my brother and sister who waited with me for the tense couple of hours during Mum's operation. By now hospital visits, check-ups, and treatments had become a very unwelcome way of life. We climbed what felt like the never-ending stairs to the surgeon's office, he had explained he would talk us through the surgery once completed. With bated breath we knocked and walked into his office. He told us all had gone very well and that he'd managed to remove Mum's uterus, ovaries, and small lurking tumours. Another victory. 3-0 to Mum. This was good! Mum was on a roll. We popped in to see Mum, hugged her, and gave her the positive news. We left her floating happily with the combination of favourable news and a cocktail of pain relief.

Mum's stay following this recent surgery was much quicker than her previous stay, it was an uncomplicated stay, and Mum was desperate to get home as soon as possible. Her surgical team felt she would repair just as well at home as she no longer needed any medical interventions from them.

It never ceased to amaze me how astonishing the human body is! Mum's body in particular. The battering it took was astounding. It never ceased to amaze me how astonishing the human soul is. Mum's soul in particular. The battering it took was astounding. Mum outwardly appeared to deal with things in a much better way than I did. It was truly humbling. She used to say that if she had this, it reduced the odds of someone she loved having it.

Following Mum's latest surgery came the final three cycles of chemo. The main health problem chemo appeared to cause for Mum was the condition peripheral neuropathy. (Peripheral neuropathy is a disorder of nerve(s), apart from the brain and spinal cord. Patients with peripheral neuropathy may have tingling, numbness, unusual sensations, weakness, or burning pain in the affected area. Often, the symptoms are symmetrical and involve both hands and feet.) Mum's neuropathy was mainly contained to her feet. She found it very painful and it could be quite debilitating on occasions. Her GP prescribed a drug named gabapentin to ease the symptoms, which generally worked. On occasions Mum's feet would give way, with little warning. She soon became good at recognising the signs in time and would, if she was inside, slide down a wall. She smiled her way through this. It wasn't this bad all the time, it appeared to come in bouts. Mum's 'C' doctor, Dr H, advised Mum that the dose of her chemo that caused the neuropathy, the Taxol part of the chemo, could be reduced significantly. Certainly not, Mum would reply. She wanted the whole deal to give herself the best chance of survival.

Mum's final three cycles of the chemo continued in a blur, posing no real concerns or threat. She required the occasional blood transfusion and magnesium infusion, but everything went relatively smoothly. It highlights what a mammoth task this was when blood transfusions and magnesium infusions become just a way of life.

Mum then had a CT scan to discover if the past few months of torment had a happy ending, this scan checked to see if all the mighty 'C' fuckers had been eradicated to Kingdom come. The wait for the results, as all previous waiting, seemed a lot longer than it was.

Again, my sister and brother and I embarked on the odyssey with Mum to receive the results. Anyone who has been in a similar position can understand the feelings. Sick to the stomach (I vomited in the morning before the appointment), legs that turn to jelly, headache, no sleep, nerves, pure nerves that take over all function and reason. Mum's GP was extremely supportive to her, he prescribed her some benzodiazepines, these are medications to reduce anxiety. I think they took the edge of the situation for Mum. She only ever took them the night before her appointments or chemotherapy.

Into Doctor H's office we trudged, keeping each other upright. The massive smile she had gave the game away immediately. "I won't keep you in suspense, you are now 'C' free," she said! Words can never explain how we felt at that moment in time. Euphoria probably best explains the feeling … jeez this 'C' disease had taken us on the roller-coaster ride of our lives. Mum had strapped in and made it to the end safely. It almost felt miraculous, I do believe that Mum's mindset had much to do with her recovery. Her determination was quite frankly humbling and never waiving. What a woman! What felt like years and years only actually took six months, and that included two major surgeries. That was only the beginning …

THE MIDDLE

Mum was now living back at home, independently. She was learning to live her life again. She had to have three monthly check-ups at the 'C' hospital to keep an eye on her. This served a double-edged sword. On one hand Mum was reassured she was being monitored, and felt a protective cocoon surrounded her, but on the other it was a constant reminder of the war she had just won. One she'd rather have forgotten about, although we both knew she could never forget it, as it still somehow managed to be there, like a soft white veil of suspicion and reminder. Mum had what is commonly known as survivors' guilt. She found it hard to work out why she had been given a second chance at life when so many people didn't have that outcome. In some ways, having 'C' is like being in a war zone (and for that reason, some oncologists argue that most 'C' survivors have some degree of post-traumatic stress syndrome). The enemy isn't a group of men, or another country, but more like a large army of 'C' cells within the body. Fear of recurrence of the 'C' was something that hounded Mum quite deeply during the earlier days of remission. Every ache or pain made her fearful that the fucker had returned. I don't think this feeling ever quite left her, she just learnt to deal with it eventually. I feel Mum felt quite lonely, not because she didn't have an army of supportive friends and family who all loved her but because unless someone has travelled the same journey how can they even begin to know or understand. I looked for support groups in Mum's area, but sadly there were none near enough. Mum told me she didn't think she could've gone to one anyway as again she felt this would be a reminder and not a comfort, for her, personally.

Mum was also trying to deal with the old bag full of shit. 'Gloria'. Initially it had provided her survival and was greeted with great relief. The reality of it turned out to be very difficult and challenging on occasions … but it had saved her life. Mum tried not to dwell on its challenges, but I know there were times when this imposition very nearly beat her. Mum grasped onto the fact that Gloria had given her a second chance when times became tough living with it. She tried to make the best of the situation and spent hours researching and buying specialised 'pretty' knickers and swimming costumes in an attempt to feel feminine once again. This did help her psychologically. You have to understand that the creation of an ostomy, whether it be an ileostomy or a colostomy, can lead to a significant change in the body image of an individual. Mum had been given the contact details of a stoma nurse assigned to her physical and emotional wellbeing. She was a very stoic character and would never ask for help unless she was desperate. She felt the professionals' time was better spent with those more in need and would rather deal with things her own way. One of the things I loved but at the same time found so sad was Mum's need to make the professionals feel better. She would laugh and joke when inside she was falling apart just to make them feel better. I'm not sure they knew what to make of this, but I do know they all adored her, they would tell me.

To make matters worse, Mum developed an allergy to the stoma bag's adhesive material. She suffered from a skin condition that was unbearably irritable and developed into a nasty rash. Mum was referred to a dermatologist and they finally found a cream she could use that didn't interfere with the sticking process. This was, however, not an instant find; Mum had to try and persevere different creams before success was gained. You can only imagine how devastating the results can be if a stoma bag cannot stick with accuracy! The other obstacle Mum found hard to adapt to living a life with Gloria was diet options, the main problem being that every food Mum loved was on the 'to avoid list' These foods tend to be foods high in fibre such as raw fruit and vegetables. Also, foods with a husk were a big no-no for Mum; tomatoes, peas, sweetcorn. Too much of these foods would cause Mum colic pain, she risked having a few dates on Christmas day and was in agony for the rest of Christmas. This was 18 months following the formation of Gloria. There was also the danger of Gloria becoming blocked if Mum ate these food groups too freely. There were of course many foods Mum could eat frivolously. We would laugh as Mum ate numerous pork pies., these became her go-to food.

When Mum had Gloria initially the Doctors warned her that it was very unlikely it would ever be able to be reversed. (An ileostomy reversal involves attaching the bowel back together allowing the individual to pass bowel motions as before surgery rather than through a stoma.) As time progressed it became more and more important for her to go back to a life without Gloria, it became an obsession for her.

Three monthly check-ups at the 'C' hospital gradually became six monthly check-ups. Mum had rediscovered her love of travelling again and went on numerous cruises with her best friend Tony. Before Mum had been diagnosed with 'C' she was due to go on a cruise up the Amazon. One of the junior doctors who had treated her when she had surgery for her bowel obstruction had given Mum her email address and told her to send a photo when she finally got to go. Mum went as soon as she was able to and she sent that photo. Mum found insurance an issue due to her now medical history but after researching found some to be very reasonable; do some research, it can be found.

During this time, my brother, Dave, and his wife Veronica had another baby, Lyla. This was what the months of torturous treatment was about! Mum got to meet her youngest grandchild, a perfect little girl, this would never have happened if she hadn't won the battle – that is a 'fuck you' to 'C'. Lyla was fittingly born on New Year's day, what a perfect start to a perfect year.

Mum's 70th Birthday was looming. Her and Tony were going on a Caribbean cruise. She also wanted to mark the occasion with family and friends. Two years before it had look doubtful she'd make that milestone. Mum decided to hold a 'celebration of life' party. It was a lovely night with many of Mum's friends and family from near and afar attending. Mum was the perfect host and revelled in the limelight. It was a truly special night. To see Mum so happy and so alive made it perfect. She had fought her way for this night, she deserved every minute of it. She glowed throughout.

That summer we enjoyed a beautiful holiday to Cuba together with Dave and Veronica and their girls. Many happy memories were made on that idyllic island.

Mum decided that she wanted any minor health concerns corrected. Throughout this middle stage she had small operations on her nose, ears, and eyes. I used to tease her by saying she had become institutionalised and could not live without some kind of contact with hospital. It baffled me that she would step back into one unless it was an emergency. Mum just wanted to live the best life she could. She would just say that these little operations were nothing compared to what she had been through.

So, we waited and waited, and we waited until finally Mum had a call to invite her in for a consultation with a general surgeon to find out if reversal of Gloria was a possibility. This was approximately a year after Dr H first planted the seed in Mum's mind. Things were complicated due to the fact that Mum was to have the operation at the hospital the ileostomy had been formed and not at her local hospital. It seemed that communications always took longer for this reason, which is understandable yet frustrating.

Mum's consultant was a tall, upright women, I shall refer to her as Miss C. She exuded confidence, which in turn filled me with confidence. She was very direct but exceedingly kind. The moment I met Miss C I felt that if anyone could do it, she could. Mum had to have a variety of tests prior to a decision being made. This, of course, dragged out the whole process, to a point I felt like Mum might change her mind.

The day came for Mum to find out if it was all steam ahead. I'm not a religious person but it was one of the days I said a little prayer. By now the nerves of Doctors appointments and the words that followed should have been second nature but that never got easier. Although this wasn't a life or death decision we were waiting to hear about, I couldn't begin to think of the effect on Mum's mental health the wrong answer would provide. I took Mum for the appointment and as we were walking into the waiting room a bird did a massive shit on me. I was plastered in it. My hair, face, and glasses all got a pounding. I remember thinking if this is good luck, I'll take it, as strangers walked by sniggering at me and my misfortune.

We were finally called in to Miss C's office. Straight to the point, she wasted no time in conveying the news we didn't dare think was possible, the old bag could be eliminated! This was one of the moments during Mum's journey that really stayed with me. The look of pure delight on her face will always be etched in my memory. She said that because Gloria had saved her life, she felt guilty about admitting how desperate she was to get rid of it, she just didn't want to seem ungrateful when others weren't so lucky. The psychological damage the big 'C' can cause is on par with the physical.

All we had to do now was wait for a date for the operation. Mum became quite impatient and would often contact Miss C's secretary to remind her she was waiting. They built quite a rapport the conversations were so frequent! At long last the date came through. Mum had already had her preoperative assessment. This had led to chats with the anaesthetist regarding concerns over her kidney function, but this had all been ironed out and dealt with. Nothing was ever completely straight forward with Mum! I stayed with Mum whilst she got ready for her operation in a little cubical. I could tell how nervous Mum was, she went into chat overdrive. The moment came for her to be wheeled down to theatre. She looked at me with a smile and uttered "I love you". She looked so small and vulnerable. I gave her a kiss and "see you on the other side" chat and off she went.

I sat in my car whilst I waited for the call to say her operation was over. I cried and cried. It was a very lonely few hours waiting for that call. Would she survive? Would the reversal be successful? These thoughts went over and over in my mind. I sat and read a book, well when I say read, I couldn't focus and ending up reading the same pages over and over and over again.

The reversal of an ileostomy usually takes 30-60 minutes. It's classed as a relatively minor operation. Mum was also having a hernia repair as she had developed a large hernia. This is quite common following an ileostomy. Having a stoma can weaken the abdominal muscles leading to a hernia.

I did not hear anything for over four hours. I was mid meltdown when my mobile phone rung. On the other end was my Mum. "Hello, I'm back and I'm just eating fishfingers and chips," she told me! I didn't know whether to laugh or cry a bit more. I had to wait another couple of hours in my car, until visiting hours, before I could see her. I could have gone home instead of waiting in my car all day. It was a 40-minute drive. I had decided not to leave as I wanted to be onsite if anything had gone wrong. Also, I was an emotional wreck. Losing Dad so unexpectedly years before made me change my whole outlook on life. It made me realise that bad things can and did happen. This shaped me into quite a pessimistic person sadly.

I waited at the ward's door at the front of the queue to be let in for visiting hours. I still didn't know how successful the operation had been, just that Mum had survived and had enjoyed her meal. I heard Mum before I saw her, she'd already got well acquainted with her fellow patients, in true Mum style. She looked so happy, that told me all I needed to know. Success had been obtained! She did also have a morphine pump,

I'm sure that had some hand in her euphoria!

Miss C popped by to see Mum whilst I was visiting her. She told us all had gone extremely well. Reversal complete, hernia repaired. Ding dong, the witch was dead!

Average time spent in hospital following ileostomy reversal is 3-5 days. Mum spent 11 days. As usual things weren't quite as straightforward for her. She endured a chest infection and various problems with her blood results just to keep everyone on their toes.

Eventually, however, I was able to take Mum home to mine to convalesce. She stayed with us for three weeks, her recovery went smoothly thankfully. Tony then picked her up from my house and took her home. He stayed with Mum for a week at her house to give her extra confidence before having to go it alone again. Slowly but surely Mum regained her confidence and felt well again. She passed her operation check-up with glowing colours. She had had no complications and the hospital were happy to discharge Mum back into the capable care of Dr H and her team. Mum took her stash of specialised ileostomy clothing in the hope that someone else could benefit without having to spend a fortune, this was typical of her, always wanting to help others.

After three and a half years, Mum was finally free of the blessing and curse that was Gloria.

So, life went on. Mum quickly began to enjoy her life; in fact, I would proclaim the next year was the happiest Mum had been since Dad had died. She really found a new lease of life. She finally settled in the area she was living in and had been living in for approximately 10 years. She joined new groups, made new friends, and was generally having a lovely time. In one aspect it was a massive relief for me. For the first time, selfishly, in a long time I didn't have to worry so much about Mum.

We chatted on the phone regularly and had regular meals together and of course plenty of shopping trips, but Mum had less time now. This, I loved. It meant that she was busy getting on with her life, a life she was determined to live to the fullest, and she did for that year.

Not long after her ileostomy reversal Mum decided she wanted to do some fundraising, in particular for the appeal linked to her oncology department at the 'C' hospital. She threw herself into her new 'project' completely and wholeheartedly. Mum had always made a variety of crafts to sell when we were younger as a way of earning some extra pocket money. They were clever and beautiful and always sold well. She decided that this was part of her fundraising plan. She spent hours and hours excitedly getting her stock together. Her idea was to hold a cheese and wine night, sell tickets for it, have a raffle, and sell her wares. She started planning this a year before it took place. She began organising the event in October 2018, she set the date for October 2019. It was so nice to see her genuinely happy and animated. I would honestly say Mum put her life and soul into her new venture. She managed to source numerous raffle prizes from local businesses. She had acquired official letters from the 'C' hospital to support her requests of prizes. People were generous and supportive. This added to Mum's glee. This event gave Mum focus and purpose.

That year we had a lovely Christmas spent at my home. Mum was in her element surrounded by her precious grandchildren. It was especially special for Mum that Christmas as she was now able to tolerate a full Christmas dinner, including all the vegetables she desired. Previous years, whilst Gloria was in situ, her Christmas dinner had consisted of meat and roast potatoes.

More importantly, now she was able to gorge herself on figs and dates without the dread of colic agony or the threat of stoma blockage. It was a really happy and jovial time. Mum left on New Year's Eve, she had never celebrated this since Dad's death, preferring to be tucked up in bed well before midnight.

Simon, my husband, our two girls Scarlett and Pippa, and I were to spend New Year's Eve at our best friends Lol and Minty's house as we had done many previous years. To save the issue of a taxi we stayed the night at theirs.

It was early hours of New Year's Day 2019. We had carried out all the usual niceties of Auld Lang Syne. The alcohol had been flowing (which in hindsight didn't help), I can remember being sat around their dining room table and just coming out with it. "This is the year my Mum's 'C' will return." Great way to ruin a lovely evening! The feeling that this was the year the fucker would resurface hit me like a ton of bricks. They all tried to reassure me that they were sure I was just drunk and over-emotional. I wasn't convinced at all. I knew from the hours of research I'd undertaken that as Mum was going into her fifth year since initial diagnosis the odds were not great in her favour. Also, I've always been a spookily intuitive person which didn't help put me at ease.

I did try to put these thoughts out of my head. Mum, after all, was on fire. She was happy and seemingly very healthy at that moment in time. "Stop being so bloody pessimistic," I would tell myself.

Mum's next six-monthly outpatient appointment at the 'C' hospital was in June 2019. I cried most of the way to pick Mum up from her house. When I arrived at the house, I had to sit in my car for a few minutes to compose myself, praying that she wouldn't spot me. I had an overwhelming feeling of dread and a gut feeling that the bastard 'C' was silent, lurking around the corner, waiting to rear its monstrous head again. I, of course, never voiced these concerns to Mum. It was a quiet dread.

The appointment went well. Mum was deemed fighting fit. The check-ups seemed so simple. Usually a set of bloods were taken. Doctor H would feel Mum's tummy and ask her how she was feeling. I actually questioned why Mum didn't have more thorough check-ups involving a scan of some kind to double check all was well. We were assured that it was unnecessary and that a negative scan could develop into a positive days after. That is how 'C' worked. I suppose it wasn't cost effective either unless there was an underlying concern. It did make sense.

When I got home that evening following the appointment, I relayed my upset and feelings of terror to Simon. He advised me that for Mum's next appointment due in December he would take the day off work and take my Mum and me to be of support. He could sense how distressed I was, and he took that seriously. He knew my thoughts of the 'C' returning that year and he also knew the year was already halfway through.

That summer Mum and Tony went on yet another cruise, this time to the Mediterranean. Mum loved cruises and the luxury they offered. Her favourite shop was situated in the town I lived in and she spent many an hour (and many a pound) on beautiful evening dresses to wear during her holidays. As always, they had a wonderful time and came back refreshed and happy with a healthy glow. Mum looked physically and psychologically outstanding! This was at the end of August 2019 … how quickly things changed.

Another cruise had been booked for later that year. It was to be a Caribbean cruise over Christmas. Mum had asked me before she had booked to see if I minded as she spent the majority of Christmas's with me and my family. I remember saying to her "go for it, you only live once". I told her we'd have a second Christmas together on her return.

Summer turned into Autumn and it was soon to be the night Mum had worked so tirelessly for over the past year. Her fundraiser. She spent the next few weeks finalising all the intricate details to ensure the night could only be a success. It made me laugh as Mum was so organised. This was not really her. She was not known for her organisational skills. Disorganised chaos that, to be fair, usually did end in success somehow. This time it was different. Everything was meticulously planned, highlighting how especially important this was for Mum, one of the most important nights of her life I'd go as far to say.

Mum had sold all the tickets for the event and sales of raffle tickets had exceed her expectations. All her crafts had been crafted and were ready to go. Finally, the night she had worked painstakingly for the past year had arrived.

We were all given our tasks for the night. Simon and Dave were designated bar men, Veronica, raffle ticket seller for last-minute buyers. Myself and my best friend Lol were in charge of the craft stall, we were kept well away from the bar. I think that was strategic of Mum! Friends of Mum had been given jobs including quiz master, games organiser, photographer ... Mum had thought of everything.

The venue was packed. Mum looked beautiful; she was radiant. Her excitement and nervousness were infectious. I felt so proud of her as she played the perfect host, floating around the room chatting happily to her guests. Mum loved her night; in fact, everyone loved her night. It was a resounding success; everyone had a lovely time. Many people asked Mum to make this an annual event as they had enjoyed themselves so much. We went back to Mum's house after the end and sat with her to count how much she had raised. It was over £3000! It was an incredibly special night; it will always stay with me. Mum planned to give a cheque to Dr H at her next check-up appointment in December, she was so happy to be able to give back to the department that had inevitably saved her life. We all went to bed that night happy and rather pissed.

I had hoped the middle part to Mum's story would last longer, a lot longer, sadly this was not to be.

THE BEGINNING OF THE END

Mum had gone to London to stay at my brother's following the months of planning her charity event. He'd moved to a new house and she couldn't wait to visit. As usual she had incorporated a full few weeks of itinerary planned to visit friends in the East of England. I had seen her the day before she went on her travels, she said she was feeling a bit low. We decided it was probably post-event blues, which was to be expected. Mum had kept herself so busy over the past year immersing herself in its organisation, I think she felt a bit redundant. I reminded her of the cruise she was embarking on only two months later and joked she had to get sorted for next year's event due to popular demand.

I will never forget the day that is now known as the beginning of the end. It was a grey and rainy October day, Monday October 28th 2019 to be precise. My daughters were on half-term holiday. We were happily watching a film whilst I was doing the ironing. My phone rang. It was my sister-in-law Veronica. She told me not to worry but she was at the hospital with Mum. Mum had by then been at their house for three days and had been admitting to pain, which meant the pain was bad and this appeared to have escalated over the days. Mum being Mum tried to dismiss this. Veronica thankfully insisted on taking her to A and E to get checked out. When I spoke to Veronica the hospital had decided to admit Mum and run some tests. They were going down the gallstone route. This made sense as a previous CT scan had actually highlighted gallstones. Mum apparently had a degree of jaundice as well, when asked if she'd noticed, Veronica told the doctors she thought it was false tan as Mum used a lotion that included a light tan. (Jaundice is a term used to describe the yellowing of the skin and the whites of the eyes. It's caused by a build-up of a substance called bilirubin.)

However much it made sense, I could not shake the nagging dread that dominated my thoughts. I told myself to stop overdramatising circumstances. I had a quick chat with Mum, she sounded quite bright and told me not to worry, she would be fine. I'm not sure she actually believed that herself, but I in turn told her of course she'd be fine.

Mum, as previously discussed, didn't like to know the specifics of any disease. This was understandable yet frustrating on occasions. Frustrating as if unless one of us were present to talk to a doctor privately we didn't really know what was actually going on. Mum would always give Doctors permission to tell my siblings and I everything. She didn't mind us knowing, she just didn't want to know herself. That in itself was hard too. Did we really want to know specifics that she was unaware of?

The roles were reversed during this period. Dave, my brother, was the nearest and spent more time at the hospital visiting Mum and being the liaison with the medical staff. I understood then how difficult it must have been for him, being so far away during Mum's last fight. You have a much fuller picture when you're there on site. Miles away you are left with your own darkened thoughts, at the mercy of someone else and the time they can update you of the latest instalments.

On the plus side, the hospital Mum had been admitted to was as lovely as a hospital can be. She said it was almost like a private ward, two nurses to a ward of six patients. Posh menu cards to pick your chosen meal from. Most importantly, all of the staff were so very kind and really looked after Mum.

That week Mum remained in hospital having various tests. We chatted daily on the phone. Dave and Veronica visited every day. Simon and I had decided if she were still hospitalised by the weekend, we would travel down to see her and give Dave and Veronica some support.

On the Thursday Mum rang me. She told me the doctors had been round. "They think it's back," she whispered. My heart almost stopped I swear. She didn't know any other details; I think she switched off as soon as they uttered the words we'd all lived in fear of. I tried to reassure her, whilst fighting back my tears.

Oh fuck, fuck! Why? Why? How? How?

I tried to convince myself not to panic, after all the doctors only thought this, there was nothing set in concrete. I decided her past medical history may have influenced their train of thought. Dave rang me that afternoon to advise me the doctors responsible for Mum's care wanted to have a conference call with him and I in the morning to discuss Mum's care and to answer any questions we might have. There were so many questions I wanted answering.

Promptly the doctors rang the following morning. Dave had advised them that I was usually at the forefront of Mum's care and they wanted to touch base with me to ensure I knew what was going on. This I really appreciated but at the same time ignorance is bliss, isn't it? That phone call was a bit of a blur, even trying to remember exactly what was discussed I find hard. The long and short of it was that they, as Mum had mentioned, felt there was a strong possibility her 'C' had returned. They were thinking it had some connection to her biliary tract (the biliary tract (biliary tree or biliary system) refers to the liver, gall bladder, and bile ducts, and how they work together to make, store, and secrete bile), there was also some mention of the pancreas being involved. They couldn't be completely sure if it was the dreaded 'C' until a biopsy had been analysed, they said. I think they were pretty sure at that point though.

Simon and I travelled down to London that afternoon to see Mum. My first thought on seeing her was just how jaundiced she did look. How long had she been like that, but we'd just not noticed? She also looked frail and was unsteady on her feet, certainly a massive deterioration from two weeks previously when she had been radiant at her fundraising event. We talked about everything except why she was in hospital. One of the doctors visited us to see if we had any questions. Mum had a habit of saying to the doctors "I'm not going to die, am I?" She asked the doctor the question that afternoon. He smiled kindly and said they would do everything they could for her. His eyes though gave everything away. I knew then at that moment in time that this was not going to have a happy ending. It hit me then the possible irony that Mum's fundraising event for the one thing that saved her life may have been the one thing to stop her seeking help earlier.

We stayed the weekend at Dave and Veronica's, making frequent visits to the hospital to see Mum, although she was physically frail, she seemed bright and outwardly positive. She was looking forward to her cruise at the end of the year, it gave her something to focus on, I think.

The hospital was a good 40 minutes' drive from Dave and Veronica's front door, even though it was only five miles from their house. That's London though! They had a hospital round the corner from theirs which luckily was the sister hospital to the one Mum had been admitted to. There were plans to get Mum moved there as it was proving a logistical nightmare for Dave, who was trying to work still and don't forget had two very small children. It was difficult though as Mum was being well looked after and was as comfortable as she could be. The doctors were kind and informative and ideally wanted to see Mum through to discharge. Nobody wanted to unsettle Mum more than necessary.

This was eventually taken out of everyone's hands though when it was decided Mum needed to have a test that could only be carried out at the sister hospital and it was to be the following week.

By now they knew something was blocking Mum's biliary tract. An ERCP was needed to relieve symptoms and take a biopsy. (ERCP stands for Endoscopic retrograde cholangiopancreatography and is a technique that combines the use of endoscopy and fluoroscopy to diagnose and treat certain problems of the biliary or pancreatic ductal systems.

It is primarily performed by highly skilled and specialty trained gastroenterologists.) They were to put a stent in place (a small plastic tube). This was to keep the bile duct open and digestive juices flowing.

So Mum was transferred to the sister hospital to have her ERCP. That happened on the following Thursday. Unfortunately, it was not completely successful as I assumed the blockage was too large. They been unable to put the stent in situ, they had not been to pass a wire into the common bile duct. This didn't surprise me as I'm sure you now realise nothing was ever straight forward for poor Mum.

Ok so that had not worked. The next plan of attack was to carry out PTC with stenting the following day. (PTC stands for percutaneous, transhepatic cholangiography – what a mouthful! (PTC is used to take pictures of the bile ducts that drain the liver. Unlike the ERCP that uses an endoscope to obtain clear images, the PTC uses the insertion of a small needle into the liver to reach the bile ducts. Once in the bile duct, a radio-opaque dye is injected into the biliary system and pictures are taken.)

Simon and I had returned to London. We had expected Mum to have had her full results the previous day following the ERCP and wanted to be there with her and Dave when the results were given. Whilst we were travelling down to London, Mum's consultant had rung Dave and told him she wanted to talk to us the following day.

None of us slept that night. We got up early and got to the hospital as breakfasts had finished. Mum's consultant hadn't given us a time and we wanted to be there for whenever she made her appearance.

The doctors started making their rounds. We sat making small talk with Mum, each of us not really paying attention to the others. Our minds were in overdrive. Eventually Mum's consultant came to Mum's bed side. She said she'd like to talk to us all privately in a side room. Alarm bells started ringing at that moment. Mum, Dave, Simon, Veronica, and myself crawled down the corridor to a pokey little room we'd been directed to. We all manged to sit, knowing deep down what was coming but that didn't prepare us in any way.

This was to be the day we were told 'that' news, the news everyone dreads, a doctor I'd never met took us into that dreadful little room. I hated her on first sight. I'm sure she was a lovely lady but, in my eyes, at that time, she was the devil. She delivered the "sorry it's back and there's nothing that can be done" speech. Mum's reaction was "bugger, bugger, shit!" Veronica said "fuck". I just sat there thinking the worst profanities but couldn't bring myself to say them out loud in front of my Mum. 46 years old and I just couldn't … instead I blurted out, "OK Mum, so what's on your bucket list?" I mean, why did I actually say that? Mum's response was "I'm going to Singapore" to which we all sat and hummed! I asked her if she'd like to go clay pigeon shooting or to the ballet? Again, why oh why? My brain and mouth had somehow become remote from each other.

I actually asked the consultant if they'd had the biopsy results back and she replied that they hadn't but were sure enough from all the findings over the past 10 days. So that was it. Game over. Mum had now entered the terminal stage. We were told it was pancreatic 'C' with liver metastases. (Metastases are the development of secondary malignant growths at a distance from the primary site of 'C'.)

They left us all sat in the room, to have some time in private, they said. Mum looked shellshocked like she hadn't really taken in the bomb that had been delivered at her feet. How was she supposed to react to news like though?

Soon after, Mum was whisked off to have her PTC procedure. Mum was now at the hospital five minutes from Dave and Veronica's house. Rather than hang around at the hospital during this time we went back to their house to try and make some sense of everything. The staff promised they would ring as soon as Mum was back to the ward so that we could get back to comfort her. We were in shock. It was difficult having Mum taken away so soon after she was given her death sentence. We all just wanted to be with her.

We sat at Dave and Veronica's not really saying much, each of us consumed in our own thoughts; I drunk Whiskey, it was 11a.m. I rung our sister Sian who was living in Dubai. I didn't have a clue what time it was or if she was at work, we just knew she had to be told. Telling her took me back to 17 years earlier when I had to ring Dave and tell him our Dad had died. Sian was obviously in shock too; she quickly regained her composure after I'd dropped the bombshell and told me she'd be on the soonest flight home she could get.

We hung around the house for a few hours and still hadn't heard anything. We rung the hospital and were told Mum still wasn't back. In the end we decided to go back and wait for her. Visiting times were 8a.m.-8p.m. so that wasn't a problem thankfully.

Mum arrived back to the ward shortly after we arrived. Luckily, the PTC was successful, and stent was now in place. Mum was so jaundiced by now; she was glowing like a belisha beacon. Mum acted like 'the' conversation with the consultant had never taken place. I think she was in denial and I didn't blame her. Mum's friend Tony had arrived. He had planned to visit anyway, and it just so happened to be 'D' day. Mum looked tired so we left them for the evening to have some private time together. We had updated Tony earlier in the day, I'm not sure if Mum even discussed it with him.

The following morning, we arrived at the hospital, again after having a sleepless night. We wanted to know an estimated timeline that Mum now had left. Mum didn't want to know, but it was important to Dave, Sian, and me. We needed to know roughly how much longer we had with our precious Mum.

We found Mum's consultant, who as predicted was sketchy. I knew from my own career it was difficult to give an accurate prediction. She told us it wasn't weeks, but it wouldn't be months either and that Mum should get her 'house in order' as soon as possible or it might be too late.

We spent the day at the hospital with Mum and travelled home in the evening. When we were en route home Dave rung us panicked to tell us the doctor from the first hospital had rung him to say how sorry he was about Mum and that he felt realistically Mum had until Christmas left. It was now the middle of November! Shit! that wasn't long enough! Panic swept through me again.

We just wanted to get Mum home from that point on. They'd found out what was wrong with her and had managed to do the procedure to keep her more comfortable, what else could they have done? The hospital said it would be mid-week the following week all going to plan. Mum was to stay at Dave's for a few days following discharge. He wanted some time with her and his little family out of the hospital environment. We would come and pick her up the following weekend and take her home. Sian would be back in England by then and would stay with her a few days before bringing her to mine to convalesce.

That is exactly what happened. The hospital discharged Mum with an urgent request to her 'C' hospital and Dr H to see Mum as soon as possible.

Mum, around this time, developed a love of McDonalds. She would have a hamburger with extra pickles and a small portion of fries. Dave sent me a photo of her eating this happily following discharge. It was the first place she wanted to visit! She looked content and excited to have escaped from the place that had just told us everything we didn't want to hear.

Dave and his family had a lovely few days on their own with Mum, enveloping her with love and kindness. That time was special for them all, I think Dave had his doubts as to whether Mum would ever return to their new home.

We arrived on the Friday night to spend a few days with them all before taking Mum home. We all found the strength somehow to have a pleasant time with Mum. The highlight for me was lying on the bed with her between myself and Lauren (my son Sam's girlfriend). I'd had a drink, which had become quite a regular occasion at that time of my life. We lay and chatted and laughed, reminiscing, divulging some of the family secrets to Lauren. It was a special evening, one that I treasure.

Sunday came and we drove Mum back home. Sian arrived, her and I spent the night at Mum's ensuring she was settled back to her beloved home comfortably. We had to do the sad task of cancelling Mum's Christmas cruise as directed by the London doctors who said she would not be medically fit to travel. That was heart-breaking, Mum thought she'd still get to go at a later date. That worried me, I wasn't sure she'd computed the damming prognosis given to her a week ago in London. I searched her face and she simply replied that she wouldn't believe anything she had been told until Dr H, her 'C' doctor, had confirmed it.

The doctors had wasted no time liaising with Dr H and there was a letter waiting for Mum when we got her home inviting her for an appointment that following week. Simon and I were to take her to this.

The following evening, I went back home and left Mum in the capable hands of Sian. It gave them a chance to have a well-needed catch-up with Sian being overseas at this time. Sian was still having to work from home during this time, but Dubai hours meant she finished her day by 13.00 hours. She could work from home, which freed up time to look after Mum.

Mum arrived at ours a few days later, ready in anticipation for her appointment with Dr H. We were all full of our own thoughts that mainly consisted of praying for a miracle of some sort. The normal 90-minute wait seemed to last at least three hours. It was horrific.

In due course Mum's name was bellowed over the loudspeaker. All I could think of was that Mum was finally going to have to confront her destiny once Dr H reinforced the previous prognosis.

The first thing Dr H said to Mum, kindly, was, "Oh poor you, you've been in the wars." I sat there thinking, 'just cut out the niceties, just get to the punch line!'

Well, inexplicably the following words she said were little short of a miracle. She told Mum that OK the 'C' was indeed back, but it was in fact treatable, just not curable! I couldn't believe what we were hearing, we'd spent the last couple of weeks subconsciously mourning our Mum. Mum looked at me as if to say 'I told you so', never have I ever been so glad to have that look before.

Mum's new treatment plan was agreed: three cycles of chemotherapy, three weeks apart, CT scan to see effectiveness of the chemo, three more cycles of chemotherapy, and then maybe the chance to partake in clinical trials. In that 30 minutes Dr H had given Mum her life back. I have never seen anyone so excited to have chemo.

I asked to speak to Dr H privately whilst Simon helped Mum back to the car. I asked her why we had been told there was nothing that could be done, and that Mum's death had been imminent by the other doctors. Dr H advised me that Mum had ovarian metastasis in her lungs, liver, and probable pancreas. She explained it was so rare to have pancreatic metastasis from ovarian origin that they must have just assumed the primary was pancreatic. Remember we were delivered the earth-shattering news without the biopsy results which may have cleared that up. Dr H said that they weren't oncologists so didn't have a specialised knowledge of this and really shouldn't have told us what they did. I had thought it strange that Mum had received no oncology input at the London hospital, we were so shocked at the time we hadn't thought to ask.

I reflected on the fact that I'd had to sit my children down and tell them Nanny wouldn't make it this time, as they sobbed at the impending loss. We were all angry the other hospital had got it so wrong, but at the same time ecstatic they had.

The journey back from the 'C' hospital was a jovial one. Mum took great delight in ringing anyone and everyone and announcing, "Ignore the rumours, I'm not dying!" It was priceless! She had a little glass of red wine when we got home to celebrate that momentous meeting with Dr H. We toasted to Mum and her new chance of hopefully a much longer life. I lay on her bed that night, she dared think of plans for the future. Her face looked relaxed now and her eyes had regained their sparkle. She knew the fight she had ahead but that didn't seem to faze her at all.

Mum equated it to a chronic disease like diabetes that just needed treatment. And yet, however much I tried, I continued to have an underlying constant feeling of dread.

Mum's first chemo was scheduled a week later. Tony came to visit and take her. Off she went nervously. He wanted to offer support wherever he could to ease some of the pressure off me. I was grateful but at the same time found it difficult transferring Mum's care into the hands of someone else. Throughout, I could never quite shake the feeling that I should be the one looking after Mum, purely selfish, I realise that now, but Mum always said she felt safe with me.

Mum's first chemo was a reduced dose of the combination drugs, Dr H had explained that this was to ease her back in gently as she had been so ill

Mum returned back to ours a few days later, Sian brought her. They had popped to get Mum's ever important nails done, to which Mum promised me she'd worn a mask as she was now at risk of neutropenia any day, making her more vulnerable to any infection. They had also stopped off to get Mum fitted for her new wig. Again, as before, this wig was remarkably similar to her own hair. She had kept the previous one but wanted to get a new wig as she had plans for the old one! She took no time in enlisting my two girls Scarlett and Pippa to 'funk' up her old wig with coloured chalks. It became multi-coloured, consisting of blue, violet, and pink streaks. Mum was delighted at this, and actually looked forward to wearing it.

The afternoon Sian brought Mum back to mine to convalesce we unpacked all her bits in the spare room. We joked that Mum had packed enough for a couple of months; Mum never was a light packer. The plan was for Mum to stay at my house for about ten days and then return home for a few days before her next chemotherapy if she felt strong enough. This was to ensure everyone some normality throughout 'fuck you 'C'' war number two.

We enjoyed a lovely couple of days, Mum had some family visitors, she enjoyed spending time catching up and chatting. I felt like the visitor guard as I would check they were in good health prior to seeing Mum. Any sign of a cold or any infection they would be turned away. This felt brutal but an absolute necessity to keep Mum as safe as possible.

I gained the confidence to leave Mum a couple of times that week so that I could go into work. Not completely confident however, as I would only go in if Simon happened to be working from home. Mum was too frail to leave on her own at this point.

I had been completing another chemo diary for Mum. We were quite obsessed with her bowels this time; past experience had left a deep mental scar. I force fed her the dreaded thermometer daily, much to Mum's annoyance.

Friday came, a week following Mum's chemo. I was going into work and checked Mum's temperature before leaving. It was initially 37.7C. Referring to the chemotherapy help card we had been given again for this cycle, it instructed me to review it again in half an hour. This I did and happily it had lowered to 36.8C. Mum said she felt fine, so I left her in the capable hands of Simon.

When I got home later that day, I did notice Mum seemed a bit odd at times. I couldn't quite put my finger on it, but I monitored her closely. It wasn't consistent, she appeared to have word-finding difficulty on occasions. We spent a quiet evening, eventually I helped Mum up to her room, we chatted for a short while and then both retired to bed.

The following morning, for some reason I was up

exceptionally early for a Saturday. I was in the bathroom and suddenly heard crashing coming from Mum's room. I ran in to find her sat in the middle of her room looking bewildered, all the drawers were on the floor with clothes scattered around. Mum tried to talk to me but instead of words I understood, it was a flow of what may have well been in Russian to me. My heart sank, something was very, very wrong.

I managed to convince Mum to let me take her temperature, it made a fast bleeping sound which alerted me it was high. Her temperature recorded 39.4C. I rang the chemo helpline at Mum's 'C' hospital. They advised me to get her there as soon as possible. I told them there was no way I would be able to get Mum down the stairs as she couldn't weight bear at all. I also reminded them that we were an hour's drive from them and I felt considering her behaviour and presentation that this was an emergency. They agreed and advised me to phone an ambulance.

Within 10 minutes an ambulance arrived. They agreed that Mum was very unwell and into hospital we were taken. Mum appeared to be more alert by then and could engage in lucid conversation.

Once we arrived at the hospital, we were taken into a side cubical as Mum was again at risk due to neutropenia. The first thing Mum asked the doctor was, "I'm not going to die, am I?"

The doctor turned to Mum and said, "The only thing I can guarantee is it won't be in the next five minutes." Blunt, but honest.

I spent all day with Mum, in that cubical. Mum was in and out of consciousness. She had periods of confusion, yet other times lucidity. The staff pumped her with IV fluids, IV antibiotics, and pain relief. When Mum was confused, it was quite happily so. I didn't know how to react to it, so just laughed. She laughed too. Inside I was terrified, as I'm sure she was too.

They confirmed Mum had neutropenic sepsis, they could not yet find the origin of it. (Sepsis is a potentially life-threatening condition caused by the body's response to an infection. The body normally releases chemicals into the bloodstream to fight an infection. Sepsis occurs when the body's response to these chemicals is out of balance, triggering changes that can damage multiple organ systems.)

After about 10 hours I could feel myself getting agitated. The main reason being that Mum was still on an uncomfortable trolley. A and E were desperately busy, in fact the whole hospital was. It was the beginning of December now, which meant higher rates of winter-related illness. I found out a few days later that had Mum been ill just a day later she would've had to go to a hospital an hour's drive due to no inpatient capacity.

The staff in A and E were very attentive, especially considering how busy they were. They spent all day trying to get Mum a bed on a ward, this was made harder due to the fact that Mum was neutropenic and needed a side room.

Finally, at 22.30 hours they found a bed, don't forget we had been at hospital since 07.30 that morning. Simon came and picked me up. I felt happy to leave Mum then, she appeared more stable.

I returned back to the hospital early the following morning. The good thing about side rooms: the staff are more relaxed about visiting hours. Usually someone is extremely unwell, and there's no disruption to the rest of the ward. Mum, however, was not a fan of side wards. She felt isolated and lonely. As discussed previously, she enjoyed a chat.

Luckily, I arrived in time to see Mum's consultant. She told me that they thought the infection leading to sepsis was in Mum's heart, endocarditis, but they weren't 100 % sure. (Endocarditis is a rare and potentially fatal infection of the inner lining of the heart (the endocardium). It's most commonly caused by bacteria entering the blood and travelling to the heart.) She advised me that time would tell if IV antibiotics would do their job and if Mum's heart was strong enough. It worried me immensely that this had been the outcome from a reduced dose of chemo, where else would there be to go? I asked Mum's consultant if she would contact Dr H, to get more details regarding Mum's medical history, she assured me she would as it would help her get a fuller picture. That was the first and last time I saw Mum's consultant.

Mum was quietly confused in bouts during the first couple of days in hospital, we all spent as much time as we could with her. Sian was still in the country and Dave even travelled down for the afternoon from London to spend a couple of hours with her, this gave a real boost.

On Tuesday a doctor I had not met before asked to speak to me. He told me then they still weren't sure where the sepsis had originated. He also made me aware it was still touch and go as they had no idea if Mum's heart was strong enough to win out.

That evening whilst I was still visiting, Dr H rang my mobile. I assumed Mum's consultant had, as discussed, contacted her. No, Dr H had no idea Mum was in hospital, she had rung to find out how things were going following her first dose of chemo. This infuriated me. I know how busy the doctors were, but surely to give Mum the best chance and to plan the best care it would have helped to be communicative with her leading consultant? Dr H told me to reassure Mum that as soon as she was well enough, she'd see her back at the 'C' hospital to form the next plan of attack together. This, again, offered Mum hope and gave her a psychological lift she needed.

The next day I was going to visit Mum in the afternoon. Her brother Simon and wife Vel were visiting in the morning. Just before lunch time my uncle rang me, "I've got some brilliant news; the doctor has said your Mum can be discharged this evening," he explained to me. I don't think he got the reaction he was expecting! I was furious and demanded to talk to the doctor on the phone there and then. He found the doctor. I asked him how they could consider sending Mum home, considering the conversation we'd had just the day before? I will admit I was so infuriated I did rant quite a lot. Eventually I calmed down and he explained to me that they felt it would be kinder to Mum now to be discharged into the comfort of our home. Of course, I wanted Mum home, I just had a terrible feeling it was too premature. I don't think they ever found the true source of Mum's sepsis, they certainly never committed 100% the origin.

My uncle was quite shocked, but said he was impressed with my no-nonsense approach to the doctor. It was out of character, but I felt passionately about the care of Mum and I felt I was living on the edge at that stage. The past week had been terrifying, maybe I just felt safer having Mum in hospital. The responsibility was enormous, and I wasn't sure I was up to that.

Uncle Si and Auntie Vel, sensing I was finding things difficult at that point, offered to have Mum at their home for a few days so that I could relax a bit. It was decided they would have Mum to stay the following few days. Mum agreed to this, she was quite excited to spend some time with her younger brother. Life had been hectic, and they hadn't spent much time together for a while.

Mum was discharged to my house which meant that we could get her organised for the next couple of days away. It worked out well as Simon and I were due to go to a music gig, this meant we could still go. We were all excited about our next few days.

I wrote a medication regime for my auntie. Mum wasn't confident in her ability to remember her medications at this time as she was still very unwell. There was a particularly humorous moment when my auntie looked horrified as she thought she'd have to inject Mum with her morphine-based liquid form medication. I reassured her whilst trying not to laugh that it was via the oral route.

Mum spent a very enjoyable couple of days away. She told me that nothing was too much trouble, she'd been waited on hand and foot. The thing she loved the most was the positivity from both my auntie and uncle. They didn't ask her any questions regarding her illness, they just spent time laughing and catching up on life. It was the perfect tonic for Mum, it helped her escape her thoughts for a while.

My other uncle, Clive, and his wife Lauren suggested they would like to have Mum to stay at theirs a few days after her return to us. This again worked out well as Simon and I had yet another gig to attend. We had resigned ourselves to the fact that we would not be able to go to either so this was an unexpected bonus. Mum was happy to do this; we wouldn't have agreed had she not been.

I must make a special mention here to Lauren. My auntie but only a few years older than me, more like a best friend than an auntie. Lauren was one of my biggest rocks throughout both 'C' journeys. She was by my side every step of the way, constantly checking how we were doing and offering help. Mum was the sister she never had, and I know Mum felt that way about her, regardless of their age difference. Lauren was also dealing with her own grief as her Dad had died a few months previously.

Mum, as with her previous visit to Uncle Si and Auntie Vel, had a lovely time. We were all refreshed and ready for whatever lay ahead. Even though Simon and I had enjoyed a few carefree days, I had missed Mum immensely and was glad to have her back home with us.

Mum, at this stage, was still very weak but utterly determined. She would insist on coming downstairs during the day, sometimes crawling down the stairs. There was a certain space on the settee reserved for her, it was nearest the door, so she didn't have as far to walk. We would bring all her bits down for her to surround her, anything she might need for the day ahead.

Mum developed little obsessions during this time. One day she was adamant she needed some knitting needles. I could not leave her on her own by now as she was just too unwell still, and I was constantly paranoid about her wellbeing. Luckily, I sent a SOS to my neighbour, who, unlike me, did have some. It was a good job as Mum wanted them there and then! She then spent the next five days just looking at them. I laughed at the urgency she had previously displayed. She just didn't have the energy to pick them up initially. Her body and mind wouldn't connect. Her mind wanted to start her newest project; her body wasn't willing.

Mum had decided that she wanted to recreate a childhood teddy bear of her brother Simon's. She had seen it at her recent visit, it was looking tired and worn, understandably following 60 years. Mum could hardly hold the knitting needles on occasions, but it became a real focus for her. It was massively important to her. Mum managed to finish all the knitting for this bear, made with much love.

Another one of Mum's obsessions was a nappy

cake she was putting together for my boss. Her baby was due early the next year. Mum sat on the floor on her knees assembling this, she recruited the help of Scarlett and Pippa as some parts were too fiddly for her weak fingers to manoeuvre.

By this phase I was working around Simon. I would go into work when he was working from home, or I'd work evenings and weekends. My job was on a bank contract, which in one respect was lucky as I wasn't contractually tied into set hours, but of course if I didn't work, I didn't get paid. My boss was incredibly supportive and did absolutely everything she could to help. My work friends became part of my salvation. Work became my sanctuary and safe haven.

Every morning, when one of us got up to start our day we would hear a voice from Mum's room, "Coooeee I'm in here," she'd tell us. This I'm sure was code for 'I'd like a cup of tea please'. Sometimes this was quite early and quite loud!

Mum's appetite was not good now. She struggled to eat a 'proper' meal. I would place some nibbles on a side plate for her to eat at her leisure. She occasionally enjoyed a small bowl of curried noodles, but that was all she could tolerate. A love of chip sticks and marmite crisps did develop. We made sure Mum had a stash of them in her room, she'd often wake in the middle of the night and eat a couple of packets. Mum, however, had lost a lot of weight, but strangely her tummy had grown, she looked pregnant. She used to joke she wished some of her tummy could be taken and stuffed in her boobs as she felt these were now 'saggy tits' she'd say.

The week before Christmas came. As Mum had been due to go on a cruise with Tony, she decided to go home for Christmas and have a quiet one with him. Luke, my nephew, would also be joining them, he wanted to be wherever she was to be. They were extremely close; Luke had lived with Mum for many years prior to spreading his wings and leaving for university.

Mum had an appointment with Dr H at the 'C' hospital, this was to discuss ongoing plan of treatment following Mum's recent hospitalisation.

The day before, Mum was in the bathroom. She asked me if I would mind shaving her hair as yet again it had started to fall out in clumps. I'd avoided this task first time round so was slightly dubious as to my hairdressing skills and my emotional strength. This was a definite laugh or cry scenario. We decided to laugh our way through the process, Mum sporting a drastic Mohican before I shaved the lot off.

Mum wore her brightly coloured wig to her appointment with Dr H the following day with pride. Scarlett, my eldest daughter at 15, had given her make up lessons at her request. Mum consistently liked to look her best and dressed up for all of her appointments. I felt a quiet pride with Mum, she was always so dignified and immaculate, however ill she was feeling. It was important to her.

The appointment with Dr H was to check how Mum was physically and psychologically. Mum had developed a strange rash to her legs, she said it had started in the hospital. Dr H took photographs as she had never seen a rash like it. Mum was prescribed antibiotic therapy for the rash to cover all bases. Dr H kindly told Mum she didn't think she was ready for another bashing from the chemo quite yet, but would see her again just after Christmas, in about 10 days.

We mentioned Mum's expanding waistline. Dr H explained this could be something called ascites. (Ascites is the accumulation of fluid in the abdominal cavity. This can be common with ovarian and liver 'C'.) It can be dealt with via a tube to drain off the excess fluid. Ascites can become very uncomfortable, causing symptoms including shortness of breath, due to space restriction for the lungs to inflate properly. Dr H sent Mum for an ultrasound to check if she'd need to have the ascites drained. The radiologist advised Mum there was fluid present but not quite enough to warrant draining at that time.

Luke was collecting Mum on his way through to take Mum home for Christmas, to spend a week in her own home with Tony and himself as planned. She was quite excited at the prospect of spending time with them and to be at her own home. Luckily, Mum had already organised Christmas much earlier, before she became ill again as she thought she'd be in the Caribbean sipping cocktails. We had planned to have a Christmas get together at the beginning of January, when Dave and his family would join us too.

The first day Mum had gone, Saturday, we had a little Christmas get together with friends, it was nice to be able to let our hair down. I had not been able to attend the numerous Christmas parties held by friends as I hadn't felt confident leaving Mum, plus I always needed to be home at 22.00 hours when Mum liked some analgesia prior to settling for the night.

I spoke to Mum on Sunday, she was bright, enjoying the company and being waited on by two willing men, Tony and Luke.

On Monday, the 23rd December, I had gone into work early. Luke rung me in a panic. He relayed the news that he had gone in to see Mum and she had been incoherent, her breathing was laboured and sounded strange. He advised me he had taken Mum's temperature and it was elevated at 39.1C. He was waiting for the on-call doctor to arrive any minute. In that moment I felt pure dismay. Not again!? Surely not! Mum had only been out of hospital for 12 days since her last admission. How much could one body endure?

I stayed on the phone whilst the doctor assessed Mum. He advised her she needed to go back into hospital, she became agitated and told him she did not want to. He told her she would die if she didn't.

An ambulance was called. It was arranged that I would meet Luke and Tony at the hospital later that day.

I left work as soon as I could and made my way to the hospital with Simon. Luke and Tony had spoken to a doctor who conveyed the little information they had so far. Mum was extremely unwell, they just needed to ascertain what exactly was going on. The conversation I had with the doctor just two weeks previously dominated my thoughts; had she been discharged too early? I don't think so in retrospect, all scenarios played out to try and make sense of what was unfolding.

Mum, on sight, looked unwell but stable. She had become incoherent again, this was how her delirium presented. We just laughed through it, more through nerves than anything else. At a later point Mum told me she knew what was coming out of her mouth was incomprehensible, she had no control over it. Frightening and in no way humorous. It gave me a very tiny insight into how the families of the people I had nursed with dementia may feel, any sympathy I had became empathy.

Mum had been placed on a ward not relevant to her condition, as beds were scarce. This proved problematic as unless any of us were present when the doctors did their visits to Mum we had no contact with them as they were in a different part of the hospital. Most of what went on during that hospital admission was relayed from Mum. As you may remember, Mum didn't want to know details as such, only if she would live or die.

Mum wasn't eating very much at all. On Christmas Eve I took her a little picnic of Christmassy nibbles to have if and when she fancied anything. She proceeded to try and smoke a breadstick (she had given up smoking 20 years previously)!

Mum decided she didn't want us to visit on Christmas Day, she was adamant about this. This was hard but I appreciated that she wanted Simon and I to have the day with our children. Luke and Tony came to us for lunch and spent the afternoon with Mum at the hospital. It was a sombre day, but for the sake of the children we did celebrate.

We couldn't be certain, due to lack of information, but it appeared that Mum had sepsis yet again. She had a severe chest infection that I assumed led to it.

This hospital stay was longer. Mum's abdomen had continued to increase in size, it had become exceedingly difficult for her to breath and it was causing her digestion difficulties.

On the morning of New Year's Eve, Mum rang me excitedly with the news that the hospital was discharging her that evening, following the drainage of her ascites.

Mums ascites drained over five litres of fluid. This took a few hours as it had to be carried out slowly to avoid a drop in Mum's blood pressure. Mum rang me whilst a doctor was with her so that I could have a chat about discharge. I told him I was concerned about time scales of hospital admissions. I asked him if Mum was likely to end up in hospital again soon, he honestly replied "yes". He also advised me that Mum would likely need to have paracentesis (draining of the ascites) again before long.

Mum finally got home to our house at 22.00 hours that night. She was jovial and in high spirits. She felt a lot better following her hospital stay that had involved numerous IV antibiotics, blood transfusion, and paracentesis. I could also tell she was relieved to live another day. She joined us for a New Year's Eve very small tipple of whiskey and even did a little jig! She was excited. It was infectious. We helped Mum up to her room before midnight.

Just after midnight we heard her voice upstairs calling to us. We rushed up to see her to be greeted by a big grin and a chorus of "Happy New Year, darlings" although I had my suspicions it would be one of worst years we would all have to endure. Sadly, my intuition is rarely wrong.

The new year, 2020, started well. Mum was still comfortable following her hospitalisation. She was, however, very weak, frail even. She liked to come downstairs for a few hours during the day. For two reasons I think; one, she enjoyed the company, and two, pure determination to prove she had life left in her still. On occasions she would come downstairs on her bottom if her legs were too weak. Stubborn and independent she would do as much as she could herself.

I had become paranoid by this stage. I think I was just waiting for the next bout of sepsis. I became obsessed with checking Mum's temperature. I tried to be subtle, but Mum could sense my fear. She would say "not that sodding thing again!" She was frightened of the result the thermometer would display, although this she would never admit.

I must have driven Mum mad; I certainly drove myself mad. Apart from shoving the unwelcome thermometer regularly under her tongue, I could hear the constant drone of my voice: "Do you have pain?" "How's your tummy behaving?" "Can you drink a bit more?" "Do you feel sick?" Mum, in all fairness, humoured me. It was difficult for both of us, she was my Mum and I had become her carer to all intents and purposes. This, I must point out, is not something I resented her for in any way, shape, or form. I did, however, resent the bastard 'C' for doing this to my lovely mum, slowly but surely sneaking her away from us all.

Another difficulty was Mum's pride. Very rarely would she admit to me if she was in pain. It was almost as if, had she not admitted to the pain it wasn't there and none of the past few months happened. Whether it was my nursing career or the fact that I was her daughter, I could instinctively tell when she was feeling uncomfortable. I would offer her regular analgesia and had the doctors prescribe it regularly rather than when required.

It was around this time regular deliveries arrived for me. Mum was obviously spending a lot of time shopping online. She said it was her way of thanking me for looking after her. Simon jokingly told me to mention I needed a new blender in front of her. Ours was buggered!

On one occasion Mum needed some crates for a project she had undertaken for Martha and Lyla. Instead of ordering the two she required, she ended up with 24! Oh how we laughed, I told her it was just "chemo brain".

It was soon Mum's next appointment at the 'C'

hospital. We were both full of trepidation over Dr H's review of Mum's recent predicament. Mum had no shoes to wear, as she'd been discharged from the hospital in her slippers. It was something we hadn't given any thought to, until that day when she needed them. Mum ended up begrudgingly wearing a pair of my boots. She was not happy as she felt they didn't go with her outfit and, as I mentioned before, appearance was paramount to Mum.

As always Dr H's immediate smile put Mum at ease. Mum was worried she'd be told her body wouldn't cope with more chemo. Dr H explained that she didn't feel Mum was quite ready to continue with her chemo journey but given time she was hopeful Mum would be able to have a reduced dose initially to ease her back in. This was music to Mum's ears. We had to make another appointment for the week later to see how things were.

That evening we received a phone call that devastated Mum. One of her oldest and dearest friends had died. They were neighbours for years; both having lost their husbands young they had been a great source of comfort for each other. Her friend had died of 'C', having been diagnosed only a few months prior. This really knocked Mum sideways, it affected her confidence too going forward.

Again, we went back to the 'C' hospital, again Dr H kindly said, "Not yet, let's give you more time to recover, I'll see you again next week". Mum's tummy had again become very enlarged, this was causing nausea. Dr H arranged for Mum to have an ultrasound scan to check ascites. The scan proved positive for ascites again, so they referred Mum to have paracentesis straight away. I sat with Mum throughout it all. I thought how brave yet again she was as I would have run a mile. It made her feel better though, which gave her the strength to endure the process.

The following week we travelled back to the 'C' hospital. To Mum's delight Dr H assured her all blood results were looking good and she would book Mum in for chemo the following week if she felt comfortable with this. Mum was excited, I was wary. She asked me what I thought. I couldn't tell her to leave it a while longer, this was the news she'd been waiting to hear. I simply told her "sometimes you have to take a leap of faith". These words I'm sure will haunt me forever more.

On an odd day that Mum felt well enough I took her out to her favourite clothes shop for a browse. My boss at work had been kind enough to loan us a wheelchair. It was the first time Mum had been anywhere other than hospital since the previous October. It finally felt safe as she hadn't had chemo for a while. We had a lovely, lovely hour. Mum bought a glamorous dress she said she was to wear on her next cruise. This I will admit broke my heart as I knew there would be no more cruises. I quietly sobbed inside, not wanting to distress Mum. Mum was happy, it gave her a little boost she needed.

One of the hardest things for me was not being able to leave Mum, as she was so unwell. This proved incredibly challenging and, as terrible as I feel and as hard as it is to admit it, it was a constant source of irritation to me. I should explain, it wasn't that Mum was a burden, and I wasn't irritated by her. I never felt that way. It was devastatingly sad and difficult when she was suffering, but we had many lovely, filled with humour kind of days. I loved that extra time I had with her and tried to make every day count. It was more frustration. If I had to go anywhere, I had to organise what we affectionately named a 'mum sitter'.

I've never been very good at asking for help. In this situation I needed people to take control. I had plenty of offers, "if you need help you just need to ask", I didn't want to ask for help, I rightly or wrongly felt it was admitting defeat. I required someone to say "this is what I'm doing for you and your Mum".

One of Mum's friends was marvellous, she'd ring me up and ask me what appointments Mum had and which she could take her to. She told me it was non-negotiable, and I had to accept help. It wasn't that I didn't want to take Mum, I wanted to be at everything. It gave me a chance to go into work. I also think it did Mum good to have a change of company periodically.

My work friends were superb too. They knew I was struggling. On one occasion I mentioned people were coming to visit Mum so I would be coming into work. They told me no I wasn't going to work; they were sneaking me out for lunch! Simon and Mum were the only ones I ever told of this. Mum said she was so glad they were looking after me and asked me to thank them from her.

This was one of the only examples of time I felt more normal during the months. It was a desperately lonely journey.

Was I ever happy? The honest answer. No. There were times, however, I could smile and laugh but was I completely happy? No, I'd have to answer, in some ways it was like a slow, drawn-out form of suffocation for both Mum and me. There were times when I could feel myself drowning in self-pity and panic. It got to the stage that I would feel sad even when Mum was happy.

My uncle Clive offered to take Mum for her chemo, she was happy with this. It was very quick, rather than the day long slog of usual. This made me realise just how little of her full dose she probably had.

Psychologically that 'leap of faith' worked wonders. The week following Mum's chemo was the best she'd been since it all began again. Her appetite came back, she was bright, and her pain seemed well controlled. I even caught her washing up on a few occasions. Mum would join us for her meals at the kitchen table, this is something she'd not had the strength to do previously.

Mum enjoyed regular visitors during this week, she was animated and a joy to be around, minus the pain and suffering of the past months.

It was also the first time I felt she was safe to leave on her own whilst I popped to work for a few hours. She texted me at work one day and simply said, "I'm listening to 'What a Difference a Day Makes' by Dinah Washington." She was excited to be finally feeling a lot better. Things were starting to improve, or so we thought at that time.

On Monday 3rd February, it was the anniversary of Dad's death, 18 years. Mum got glammed up and we went out to a local garden centre that she always enjoyed visiting. We perused the gifts and plants on offer and had lunch in the little restaurant. It was special time. We raised a glass of orange juice to Dad. Mum was vibrant and happy to be out, albeit in the wheelchair as her legs were still weak.

The following day Mum left my house. She was to spend a few days at her home as Simon and I had booked a trip to Amsterdam months previously. She wanted us to still go, saying we needed it more than ever. Tony had kindly offered to look after her. I sent Mum with a list of contact numbers, steps to carry out in the event of any health concerns, an inventory of all drugs Mum took and when.

Simon drove her to her house to await Tony. I was going to work. We left at the same time. I came back, I didn't make it to work. I was completely overwhelmed with feelings of utter despair. I, like Dave previously, had a strong feeling Mum would never return to my house.

THE END

It took me longer to pluck up the courage to start writing the end than it did to write everything previously. Maybe it was still so raw, maybe I was at the denial stage and I couldn't bring myself to tell this part of the story. It was all so final; the end meaning 'conclusion', 'termination'.

So, Mum had excitedly gone back to spend a few days at her home whilst Simon and I had a short break to Amsterdam, to go to a gig of one of our favourite music artists. Mum left on the Tuesday. Thursday was her birthday and the day we were due to fly.

My uncle Clive popped by to see Mum at her house on the Wednesday, the day after she had left my house. He rung me after seeing her and told me he was worried about her as she was still in bed and didn't appear to recognise him initially. Although this had been the reality of Mum's life over the past few months, I rang her to investigate how things were. She laughed and told me she thought Clive would contact me to snitch, but that she was fine, she had been resting and was disorientated as she hadn't expected to see him. I felt reassured. On reflection that was a massive mistake.

The following morning, I rang Mum on the way to the airport, to sing Happy Birthday and to check she was doing OK. Mum sounded bright and exhilarated. Tony was taking her out for lunch, she couldn't wait to get out and about, albeit being pushed around in her wheelchair.

I felt comforted talking to Mum and let my hair down. Simon and I had a great time that night in Amsterdam, making the most of our time alone in one of our favourite cities.

It was late, or should I say early morning, by the time we got to bed, as obviously it was Amsterdam!

Early that morning, about 8.30, my phone rang. Miraculously it woke me up from my alcohol-induced slumber. It was Tony, oh fuck, what was wrong? I thought through my pounding headache.

Tony was very calm. He told me Mum had endured a bad night and was not making any sense. My heart sunk. The first thing I asked him was what her temperature was? He hadn't checked by then but said he would ring me back when he had. After what seemed liked hours but was only five minutes Tony rang back and informed me it was 39.6. I told him to ring an ambulance as this had a very déjà vu feel about it. I rang a friend of Mum's, Alison, who was a retired nurse and asked her if she could go and be with Mum and Tony. This was to give Tony some support and to provide another head on the case.

Tony rang me a while later to say the ambulance had arrived. The paramedics had assessed Mum. They weren't overly concerned but would take her to hospital as a precaution due to her past medical history. Tony said he would keep me updated, not to worry too much and try and have a nice day. Alison said the same. I spoke to Mum when she was on transit to hospital and she seemed relatively lucid, far more so than previous admissions. Tony told me the hospital felt she would be discharged the following day.

Simon and I tried to have a good time, and we did for the most part but of course there was an underlying apprehension of fear. Tony kept in contact, told us there was no need for us to fly home early and that Mum was stable and comfortable. The hospital was undergoing tests to find out what the cause of the latest drama was. I in turn had updated Dave and Sian.

We flew back on Saturday. I spoke to Mum. She told me she didn't want us rushing to the hospital. There was an extreme storm, she said it would cause her worry, she'd see us on Monday when the weather was forecasted to be calm again. I advised Mum that I needed to see her, she refused, this was something she had never done before.

Tony had returned back to his home by now.

On Monday Simon and I made our way to the now all-familiar hospital. Mum had been put in a side room as she was so unwell. She appeared slightly confused but overjoyed to see us. I spoke to a nurse to find out what was going on, it was all a bit sketchy at that stage, but it appeared to be sepsis yet again. My main worry was would Mum ever be able in all reality to have chemo again?

Over the next couple of days, we went backwards and forwards from home to hospital. The doctors found the source of the sepsis, it was a blood infection caused by e coli. (Escherichia coli is a type of bacteria that normally lives in your intestines. It's also found in the gut of some animals.) Most types of E. coli are harmless and even help keep your digestive tract healthy. Because Mum was immunosuppressed it escalated. I couldn't think of how Mum had developed this. She was hardly eating, and my household were overly vigilant with infection control when Mum was neutropenic. The doctor reassured me that it had been nothing we had done, it just highlighted just how ill and vulnerable Mum actually was.

Mum was seriously ill. She required yet another magnesium and blood transfusion, this had become standard. She also had a potassium transfusion, that was a new one. She was extremely confused by now.

Dr H rang me, I had advised her secretary of Mum's recent admission. Dr H was not her usual positive, happy self. She was able to access Mum's notes from the hospital admission. She admitted to me that even if Mum made it out of hospital, she would not be able to have chemo again. This was the news I had known deep down but feared the most. Until Dr H confirmed it, there had been hope. Hope was slipping away quickly now.

Dave had joined me by then from London. We were both staying at Mum's house as it was a 10-minute train journey. Neither of us were in the right frame of mind to drive, let alone deal with the stress of trying to park once there. Mum's doctor had advised us both not to go far.

By the Thursday the doctors felt they had finally found the correct antibiotic to treat Mum. She was much more coherent. Something in Mum's mindset had changed though. She appeared defeated. She never voiced it, but I know she realised herself that there could be no more chemo now moving forward, she was in a terrible place mentally, I had never seen her low. It was like a quiet resignation.

Mum had by now been moved into a bay with five other ladies. This suited her as she liked to have a chat and a nose at what was going on.

On the Friday Dave and I were advised by Mum's doctor that she was responding well to the current antibiotics now, and they even mentioned the possibility of discharge early the following week. Dave and I looked at each other astonished when they stated this. Yes, she appeared stable by then, but in our minds a long way off from being strong enough to leave her home for the past week.

Dave went home that night, to return on Monday. I went home to see my family.

Simon and I visited Mum on Sunday. I was worried as she wasn't answering her mobile phone. This usually indicated things weren't quite right, either she felt too unwell or was confused and couldn't compute the ring of the phone. This happened a lot during Mum's hospital admission.

When we got to the hospital Mum remained confused, but happily so, I couldn't get it out of my head that they had hoped to discharge her a few days later. On our way out, following visiting, I mentioned to a nurse I wasn't happy as Mum seemed more confused than ever. She looked surprised but assured me she would check and get the doctors involved if necessary.

The following day was Monday 17th February. I had a phone call from Mum's doctor, Dr L. The minute I heard her voice I knew the news wasn't positive. Doctors didn't make a habit of ringing. She told me she was so sorry to tell me over the phone but advised me to get to the hospital as soon as possible. There was nothing that could be done for Mum now. Dr L advised me that if Mum didn't respond to yet more, different antibiotics she had hours, if she did it would just be a matter of days.

I knew Dave was on his way back anyway and didn't want to alarm him whilst he was en route. Simon was still at work (his work took him around the country). My auntie and uncle came and picked me up and took me to the hospital. I rang Sian in Dubai; she immediately booked a flight that would land the following morning.

The staff on Mum's ward had become like family, we had spent so much time there with Mum. They were so kind to us all and accommodated us well around the strict visiting hours. One of the nurses told me they all loved Mum.

Mum still outwardly hadn't been told what we had. I think she could sense it, and obviously she was the only one who truly knew how she felt physically. Sian had flown back from Dubai by now, it was obvious it wasn't good. Mum had a stream of visitors, including all her grandchildren. Tony, after being informed of Mum's imminent prognosis, had also returned. By now I was staying back at Mum's house with Dave,

Tony, and Luke.

Wednesday 19th February it was decided Mum had another infection on top of her original. It was a bad day as the doctors decided to tell her that she would not be able to have any more chemo (when none of us were present). This was something we had protected Mum from knowing, as she didn't want to know. She looked me in the eye and asked me to tell her the truth. She asked me what Dr H had said and asked me if she felt the same way regarding the chemo. In a split second I had to decide whether to lie or tell her the truth. I don't know if it was the right thing to this day, but I told her the truth. She just shrugged her shoulders and said, "Ok well that's that then." At that moment in time my heart shattered into pieces, maybe never to fully mend again.

We were spending all day at the hospital now, taking it in turns to sit with Mum. As she was still on the main ward, practically we were unable to all be there at once. This proved frustrating as we all knew time was running out and we all wanted to be with Mum as much as humanly possible. The ward was trying to find Mum a side ward which would mean we could all be with her all day and night if we wished. They wanted to keep Mum on their ward to allow continuity of her care. This was what we wanted too, Mum knew the staff well by now and we had built a good rapport with them. We were told Mum's metastasis in her liver were massive now.

Dave, Sian, and I decided to go for lunch to a pub around the corner from the hospital to talk about funeral arrangements. As you can only imagine this was a very emotional lunch. It was also a very boozy lunch. It was the only way we could crawl our way through the details. We finally set a plan. It was something that needed to be done, yet at the same time we all felt a sense of betrayal to Mum, who was lying in a hospital bed still unaware as far as we could tell that her life was fading fast.

By the time we finished our lunch it was 4-ish. We decided to swagger back to the hospital to see Mum before retiring for the night. I must add, shamefully, I don't remember much about the next part, it was conveyed back to me from Dave. Apparently, Sian and I got into bed with Mum, smothering her with our love, which she loved! I then proceeded to get out of bed and puke all over the hospital floor by the side of her bed! Never have I ever been so mortified. Dave jokingly said I was incredibly quiet and that he and one of the care assistants quietly cleaned it up. Luckily, Mum had her curtains around the bed permanently now, so at least the whole ward didn't witness the whole spectacle. I found some comfort in that. Sian spent the whole night being sick at her house, at least she was dignified enough to do it privately.

Monday 24th February was a day I will never forget for as long as I live. Sian and I were sat with Mum and the palliative care doctor popped by to see her. (Palliative care is an approach that improves the quality of life of patients and their families facing the problem associated with life-threatening illness, through the prevention and relief of suffering by means of early identification and impeccable assessment and treatment of pain and other problems, physical, psychosocial, and spiritual.)

The palliative care doctor was a lovely lady and very personable. Mum was now admitting to being in more pain, I knew it had to be intense for her to admit this. The doctor said she would prescribe a syringe driver for Mum and mentioned the possibility of a hospice. With those few sentences Mum became panicked. The look on her face will stay with me and Sian, I'm sure, for ever more. It was almost like 80% of the life Mum had left at that point drained. She looked like she was internally convulsing at the information just shared with her. We held her to offer reassurance. She kept saying over and over, "I'm not ready to die, please don't let me die, I've still got so much I want to do."

We told Mum we would get her home if that was what we wanted. Mum didn't want to go home to die, she said she didn't want to put us through that. We all reassured her if that's what she wanted that was what we would do, but still she declined. In hindsight it was a blessing. In hospital Mum had pain relief at the press of a bell. I did wonder if she thought that she was being sent home to die and that's why she resisted. Maybe she thought if she stayed in hospital, she'd still have a chance.

We were all now suffering from what is known as anticipatory grief. (Anticipatory grief refers to a feeling of grief occurring before an impending loss. Typically, the impending loss is the death of someone close due to illness.)

That night we all sat around her bed side. She seemed to have lost the will to live there and then. We were frightened to leave her in case anything happened. Sian, Dave, and I had all made a pact to be with her at the end. Mum sat upright in bed at about 23.00 hours, asking where her brother Clive was. We rang him, him and his wife Lauren made the 50-mile journey over. We spoke to the nurses who at 03.30 advised us to go home, they said they didn't feel anything would happen that night and would ring us immediately if there were any problems. One of the nurses kindly reassured me that it made no difference that I was a nurse, she was my Mum. She told me her Mum had died in similar circumstances and she, like me, had no gauge on events. I felt I should know exactly how long Mum had left, Dave and Sian looked to me for guidance and I couldn't give it.

From that day on, Mum kept drifting in and out of consciousness for long periods. It was almost as if her brain was trying to protect her from the news of her impending death.

The doctors had finally discontinued her IV antibiotics. Mum's arms were like pin cushions. She had been restless and kept pulling her cannulas out. (Intravenous cannulation is a process by which a small plastic tube (a cannula) is inserted into a peripheral vein. The subsequent venous access can be used for the administration of fluids, medication, and nutrition.) We asked them to stop re-cannulating Mum as it was causing her so much distress and discomfort. They finally agreed. The hospital did everything they possibly could for Mum, no one could ever fault them.

When Mum was conscious, we had many chats. She would ask forgiveness for doing this to us all. I told her how sorry I was we didn't beat it this time. We had time to tell Mum how much we loved her and to thank her for everything, something we had been cheated of when Dad had died.

There were humorous occasions. Mum would say she wanted a burger with extra pickles. As she was hardly eating, we jumped at the chance to get her some substance. Dave and I walked many miles for those precious burgers and quite often she'd have just one bite.

The ward had managed to find Mum a side ward, this proved great relief to us all, it meant we could all be together with Mum for as long as we needed.

Some days, all morning Mum would be unconscious whilst Sian, Dave, and I held vigil beside her bedside. Simon would walk in the room and she would sit up with a big grin on her face. Sian, Dave, and I would look at each other and just shrug.

Mum declared on one occasion that she wanted plenty of people at her funeral. I think that was her way of telling us that she had accepted her fate. She told me one day she was ready to be with Dad again, then five minutes later she retracted this statement.

Mum also told Sian, Dave, and I she wanted lots and lots of flowers at her funeral and that she didn't want donations of any kind. This threw me a bit as a) Mum had always found flowers sad as they died so quickly, she preferred garden plants and b) she had spent her last healthy year fundraising nonstop. However, these were her wishes so we promised we would grant them for her.

One afternoon Mum asked us to list all the people other than Dad and her Mum and Dad she'd be reunited with on the other side. She smiled at the thought of sharing a sherry with Judith her dear friend who had died so recently. It was sad the list we were able to give her, it really was quite long.

The palliative care team were spending time with us. They were incredibly supportive of our emotional needs and made adjustments to Mum's drug regime as needed.

We were by now wishing Mum away, to relieve her of her suffering and to relieve us from having to watch it any longer. That felt such a horrible thing to do but at the same time it just seemed kinder by then. Mum, however, clung on to life with her ongoing determination. One of the nurses told us she'd never known anyone fight death so much in her whole career.

They told us about the hospital chapel. I was not religious, but the nurse told us it was a nice quiet place to gather thoughts. I made my way up to the Chapel when I needed some peace.

The minute I walked in I felt an overwhelming sense of serenity. It felt like being wrapped in cotton wool. I was able to write a message about Mum on a ribbon and leave it entwined with the numerous others in a collage. I found the half hour I spent sat peacefully of great comfort.

Tuesday 3rd March. Mum had been quite bright the day before, she had asked for drinks on numerous occasions and had joined in conversation. The 3rd was a different story. Dave and I got to the hospital quite early. Mum was unconscious and non-responsive.

Sian joined us, we all sat with Mum until Luke arrived at lunchtime. Luke was going back home later that day, a 150-mile drive, we left him and his girlfriend Emma to have some private time with Mum. We went to have some lunch. We'd only been from the hospital an hour when Luke rang. He told us to get back quickly as the nurses were concerned that Mum's breathing had now changed. We all ran back. Mum's breathing had changed, I knew then that would be the day that Mum would die.

Luke and Emma left.

Sian, Dave, and I cocooned Mum. We made sure she had her favourite music playing, her favourite scent, white musk filled the air and we didn't leave her side. We bared our souls to her whilst there was still time, not knowing if she could hear us. The rest of that day shall remain private and encapsulated within my soul forever.

Our darling Mum finally lost her courageous fight at 22.35 on Tuesday 3rd March 2020. A light went out inside me that day. Something inside me also died that night.

THE AFTERMATH

Sian, Dave, and I went back to Sian's for the night as she lived round the corner from the hospital. We all wanted to be together at that time. We were shellshocked after the ordeal that had unravelled in front of our eyes earlier. We sat up for a bit, drinking in a numb state, making a few important calls to be made that late at night.

The following morning Sian went into project manager mode and set about sorting the funeral out. Dave got the train back to London as he was desperate to see his little family after a month of being away from them all. Simon came and picked me up. I, too, had been away from my family for most of the month.

I had taken on the task of ringing around and breaking the sad news to the entire contents of Mum's address book. That wasn't a nice task, I found it odd, I was apologising to everyone. People reacted in different ways, someone hung up on me, another person screamed and howled hysterically.

Sian had registered Mum's death and had set a date for Mum's funeral for Tuesday 17th March. She was due to fly back to Dubai the day after. We were mindful Mum had requested a lot of people at her funeral, this was to prove more stressful than we realised at the time as Covid-19 lurked around the corner.

Everyone had started to become nervous about the inevitability of coronavirus hitting our shores.

Being back at home was a challenge in itself. It felt like a black hole. Mum was missing from the chair she'd kept warm for so many months, and how I longed for just one more "Coooooeeee I'm in here" to wake everyone up in the morning.

We had become slightly institutionalised having spent the past month at hospital. Staff had become our extended family and friends, hospital our home.

I missed the walk up the stairs or cramming in the lift that took ages to come. I missed the extortionate coffee shop. I missed the staff and routine. I missed the smell of hospital air. I missed my brother and sister. I missed our Mum and all that she had taken with her.

Sian, Dave, and I were now orphans. That itself was difficult to compute. The two people who loved us unconditionally like no other had exited our lives, leaving us vulnerable and at a loss with the world. We were all still relatively young, Dave being only 40 at the time.

The days between Mum's death and her funeral were a blur. I kept myself busy arranging photo presentations and boards to include at the wake. The messages of condolence flooded in; these were comforting. It was nice to have reinforcement of so much love for Mum.

I ordered packets and packets of Forget Me Nots for Mum's wake, I felt these could be given to everyone in attendance to scatter in Mum's memory, I will come back to this later on.

Sian had chosen well with the funeral directors. No one could have done more for us, they did it in such a sensitive way too, making the whole process more bearable than it could have been.

Monday March 16th came. It was the night before the funeral. We were to stay at Mum's house with Dave, his family, and other members of the family.

Covid fear had set in by now, many mourners had decided to stay away if they had underlying health concerns. This we completely understood, but we were worried no one would turn up and our promise to Mum would be shattered.

Dave and I decided to go to the chapel of rest to see Mum. Dave had already been earlier in the day but wanted to go again. This was something I didn't think

I wanted to do but I'd been having nightmares over the last few hours spent with Mum and I hoped it would clear my mind of that, eradicate those thoughts. Simon drove us.

The funeral directors knew us by then, we were sat in a little lounge, full of bottles of alcohol of all descriptions. They told us to help ourselves and work our way through them. Dave and I did a rather good job of following the brief! Mum would've expected nothing less from her two youngest. It was all in her honour you understand.

Sian and I had previously sent Mum's favourite dress and shoes for her to wear on her final voyage. I didn't spend long with Mum, it all felt like a dream, but I'm glad I did it. She looked peaceful. Her tummy that had struggled so tirelessly with ascites, was now flat. Mum would've been happy with that, that in turn gave me some peace.

Mum's funeral the following day turned out to be as perfect as saying goodbye to someone we loved with all our being could be. She would've loved her special day, of that I'm convinced. Our concerns of a lack of mourners was unfounded. The church was full. There was a mass array of beautiful flowers, predominantly of daffodil origin as these had been Mum's favourites. The service was personal, warm, and loving. I really hope that Mum would have been proud of us all.

Mum's wake followed at a local pub she used to frequent with her Mum. It had become a favoured place for Mum over the years. Mum's wake was lively and full of love. It really was a celebration of a wonderful, beautiful life.

The day after Sian flew back to Dubai and Dave went back to London. We were all left to rebuild our lives.

We were very lucky, if that's the correct term. Covid-19 had started sweeping the nation. Just six days after Mum's funeral the whole country went into full lockdown. We often spoke about how horrific it must have been for poor souls dying alone in hospital and the devastation it must have caused family members left behind. Funerals, too, quickly became extremely minimal in numbers allowed to the service. It was all beyond comprehension. We had escaped such a predicament, just!

Once the funeral was over, life went on for everyone else, albeit a new way of life in the unprecedented times upon us. Covid-19 became an extension of our grief. I for one hadn't seen most of my friends properly since the previous November when Mum's illness had returned. I had really been in lockdown since then.

Life wasn't normal, so how could we grieve normally? There was nothing to look forward to amongst the darkness. No holidays, festivals, music gigs, family and friend get togethers, nothing to slightly ease the pain we were suffering. This I know; Sian, Dave, and I all struggled with it. I at least could carry on going out to work as a key worker. They both tackled the isolation home working brought them on top of everything else.

We had regular group Zoom calls to keep in touch during the newness of our grief. Mum had named us all executors of her will. Dave took on the combined role of this. It was difficult for Sian being in Dubai and I was no help with things like that. A hard task for Dave, made even harder as so many workplaces had furloughed staff throughout the pandemic. Getting hold of certain people proved testing during that time. We had Mum's house to sell but decided it might be wiser to hang off until the housing market reopened following lockdown.

Time passed in slow motion. Mum was the first thing I thought of in the morning and the last thing I'd think of at night. There are many stages associated with grief. They are feelings that may or may not occur:

Feeling numb: not reacting to the event. Feeling everything is normal. This usually occurs if the death was unexpected or a traumatic event.

Personally, I didn't think numbness was prevalent. I look back now and it probably was, even though it was expected, the events had been extremely traumatic.

Denial: difficulty in believing the person has gone and won't be coming back ever. Denial is a common reaction to grief and manifests subconsciously. A table may be set for the person who has died. Ringing the person to hear their voice, expecting them to answer the phone.

Yep this emotion was present. I would lie on what had been Mum's bed in our home and cuddle a pillow pretending, longing it to be her. I often texted Mum's phone asking when she was coming back.

Acceptance and relief: when someone has endured a long and distressing illness, there may be feelings of relief that their suffering has finally ended. Anticipatory grief may help prepare for the actual event.

Relief was one of the first emotions to hit me. Mum had suffered so much. We didn't have to see the fear in her eyes and listen to her pleads to save her anymore.

Yearning and searching longing for someone who has died can become a physical feeling, and this can hurt immensely. You may believe you have seen the person, to find they just have the same hairstyle or be wearing the same clothes.

I longed to see Mum again. I never felt I saw her

physically, but I became obsessed with white feathers.

White feathers symbolise faith and protection. There is a saying, "when feathers appear, angels are near." I found lots of white feathers in the initial months after Mum died, this bizarrely I found a real comfort. When I finally saw Dave again, I asked him if he had to which he replied no. I remember saying, "I'm OK, Mum, Dave needs you now." When Dave got home he sent me a photograph. His back garden was covered in white feathers!

I had asked Mum before she died to knock over a plant pot to communicate she was there, this I am still waiting for.

Repeating the event: going over and over the events in your mind. Talking to others may be helpful in accepting what has happened.

This I did a lot. I had no problem conversing about the event. I bored myself.

Restlessness and disturbed sleep: you may not be able to relax your mind of the events occurring, leading to disruption in your ability to rest well and sleep properly.

This happened to me more during the anticipatory stage. We would leave the hospital at night and expect a call to get back as soon as we could. I didn't sleep properly for that whole month.

Once I had visited Mum in the chapel of rest, my sleep returned to a relatively normal pattern.

Loss of confidence: this can manifest due to lots of different reasons. Watching someone you love die can make your confidence in your own health deplete. If your partner dies you may have lost the yin to your yang, the person who made you complete. You may feel people expect you to be through the grief process which will in turn dent your confidence levels.

My confidence was affected massively; I found larger groups more difficult to deal with, developing moments of anxiety at the most unexpected times. I developed ongoing confidence issues with my own health.

Guilt: you may have feelings of guilt about your relationship with the person who died. Things that were said or unsaid. Guilt may be present if you felt something more should have been done for the person, if you were older than them, or ill yourself.

I had many feelings of guilt. Why had I told Mum to take that leap of faith? Could more have been done for her? If I hadn't gone to Amsterdam, would she have been OK? Why did I always force that thermometer at her? Why did I nag her constantly to eat and drink? Grief is a very selfish embarkment that really only those that have travelled can identify with. I felt guilt that I was relieved when Mum had died and so it went on.

People tried to reassure me that I had nothing to feel guilty about, but it's a feeling that didn't go away and something I learned to live with.

Anger: this can be directed at anyone: health professionals you felt didn't do enough, friends and family you feel didn't do enough for the person who died or enough to support you. The person who died, how could they have left you? Why didn't they fight a bit more, a bit longer?

Anger is another emotion I found overwhelmed me on occasions. Simple things would escalate in my mind. This response was unfamiliar to me as I was not generally an angry person at all. I had many a rant in the earlier months. I was angry with the whole world and everyone in it at some stages.

Profound sadness and depression: in the weeks immediately after the death, you will probably receive a lot of support and sympathy, but this might wane as life goes 'back to normal' for people who have been less affected. This, however, is often not the case for those living with grief, your whole life may change completely, never to be the same again. The devastation of missing the person you've lost and maybe your whole identity can cause profound sadness and may lead to depression. If you feel depressed, or need extra support, contact your GP or a specialist person or organisation to help get bereavement support.

I felt profound sadness but luckily never depression.

As aforementioned I had brought packets of Forget Me Nots to share at Mum's funeral. I obviously wasn't firing on all cylinders and many came home with me. A couple of months later I decided it would be a nice idea to have a 'Mum's memorial garden' in an area with some trees. Me being me thought we just had to scatter them, I enlisted the help of Scarlett and Pippa and we spent ages lovingly scattering the seeds.

A couple of months went by and I started to receive pictures of lovely blooms of Forget Me Nots. This I found odd as I checked mine regularly and there was no evidence of life. It was then a friend asked me if I had covered them with soil! Hmm no we just scattered them, obviously the birds had a field day!

Mum would've laughed at me as this was typical. I have never been known for my green fingers. She used to buy me a poinsettia just before Christmas every year without fail. It would be lucky to make it to the new year.

Something that was said to me about three months after Mum had died rung true. "No one seems to understand, especially as most haven't been through it. No one asks if you're alright anymore. Just got to get on with it." I could relate to this, but on this note I'd like to make a special mention to Lol, my best friend.

Mum always said she was like a surrogate daughter to her, having known her for many years. She was the one who visited me regularly when I couldn't leave the house for days on end when Mum was so ill. She was the one who messaged daily just to see how things were, or if she could help in any way at all. She's the one who listened to me without judgement once Mum died. I will never, ever forget what she did for me.

I learnt a lot about myself following Mum's death. Sadly, I also learnt that I don't have many real friends. Friends I had cherished for years, I felt at that time abandoned me. I'm not laying blame as it must have been hard for them, but then again it was hardly a bed of roses for my family and I. I felt I became alien to them overnight, how odd, but to be fair I became an alien to myself. I was lucky enough to have a lovely group of friends who did look after me.

A friend who had lost both parents summed it up perfectly, he said not many of his friends had lost one let alone two parents at our age so how could they begin to relate. Of course, we know how it feels so we will know and understand their heartbreak when sadly that time arrives, which inevitably it will.

Largely I found myself gravitating to a very small

handful of friends who had lost a parent, they are the only ones who can truly begin to imagine the horror that faces you.

It took a while to have access to Mum's ashes due to lockdown restrictions and this bothered me. Mum had left us strict instructions. She wanted to be mixed with Dad's ashes, some placed at the churchyard of the village we grew up in and the rest scattered over the reservoir she was born at, her happy place she'd say. Although the ashes weren't mixed immediately it was a great relief to collect her and stand her next to Dad (his ashes) once again. We jokingly place them in our home garden bar and placed a glass of whiskey by their side.

Four months after Mum had died, we were finally able to get her house on the market. To our astonishment it sold after just 12 days of being live. We had all prepared ourselves for a long wait, as the housing market had suffered due to the pandemic. People were nervous about moving and investing in property, due to the economic ramifications the country faced. This emotionally was a boost. Mum had loved her house so much that to sell it to the first person to enter it was such an unbelievable feeling.

What it did mean was the house now needed to be packed up. This was a job none of us relished the thought of.

Sian was still residing in Dubai and unable to fly in and out. Dave was in London with his small children. Simon and I took on the project.

Initially I found the task heart-breaking. I'd visualise Mum in every room. It just felt intrusive. Who were we to decide what was to be kept or tossed into a skip? This played on my mind, eventually we had to be practical. There were many things I couldn't bring myself to discard, so they went straight into our loft at home. I spent hours going through every drawer and crevice. I didn't want to accidently lose anything that had been precious to Mum. It was painstaking, a meticulous labour of love.

Mum lived in a fairly large four-bedroom detached house, so it wasn't a quick job. It took longer as I felt we owed it to Mum to treat everything with the respect it deserved.

I had lots of offers of help with the packing up, the problem was I wanted to oversee it all. I knew the treasures of Mum's heart. I knew the little pair of plastic football boots were given to her on their wedding day from Dad, someone else might have tossed them aside. I knew all the memories attached to certain knickknacks of Mum's that might otherwise have ended up in the rubbish. I wanted and needed to be in control of the whole process from beginning to end, I felt I owed that to Mum, it was the last thing I could do to honour her memory.

Sorting out Mum's clothes was the thing I personally found the hardest. I sat on the floor in her room filling black bin bags with her vast wardrobe. I apologised to Mum during every drawer I emptied with tears rolling down my cheeks. We donated Mum's clothes to a hospice charity, I thought she would approve of that.

I learnt two things about Mum packing her house up ...

1) She had clothes, hundreds, of clothes with labels still in, Mum would have been laughing at me cursing her.

2) Mum's ability to weld everything to the walls; pictures, mirrors. These all took much manoeuvring to remove whilst leaving the walls intact.

Life went on, naturally it had to. I knew from losing Dad that it doesn't get easier, you just learn to live with 'it' somehow. A lot of people seemed to have a limited supply of sympathy. I found myself, after five months, telling everyone that I was now OK and at peace, yeah right! It was almost as if that was the expectation, one I wanted to fulfil. In reality of course those who loved me wanted to hear I was doing OK, but the depths of my despair ran deep.

Life became a different normal. A life without Mum in it was hard to navigate.

There was no one left to ask questions about our

history and heritage now. There was no one to stitch the hem on my curtains that dragged on the floor. There was no one who could bake anything from scratch quite the same. There was no one whose home was quite as welcoming again. There was no one who could chat quite as much anymore, how I missed her constant talking. There was no one left to buy us quirky Christmas presents. There was no more Mum and her love and embraces that somehow made everything seem so much better.

Losing Mum definitely changed me, more so than the loss of Dad. It was the end of that line, to be honest on occasions just the thought was unbearable.

I found myself distancing from certain friends and large social situations became difficult, anyone who knew me knew this was not normal. Luckily, things were easier to avoid due to Covid-19 restrictions initially. I felt no one really wanted to be around me, which was ridiculous, and really not fair, maybe that stemmed from the feelings of abandonment I had felt earlier on. I found a subtle hint of paranoia had crept into my fragile mind. Anxiety kicked in; this was alien to me. Feelings of complete desperation became the norm.

I became impulsive, leaving a job I had been in and loved for the past 12 years.

Intolerance became a major player in my life,

combined with impulsiveness, this proved challenging. It hit home to me that you only live once so don't take any crap. I maybe took this too literally.

My world became very black and white for a while. There was no in between.

I spent many waking hours convincing myself I had 'C', that was the reality. The enemy 'C' can leave a trail of destruction impregnated in the minds of those left behind, with no real respite from those dark thoughts.

If I had tooth ache, I had mouth 'C', tummy ache I had a gynaecological 'C', if I had a headache, yep it was a brain tumour in my mind. Once your world has come crumbling down thanks to 'C' it's very hard to claw your way back into the sunshine and reality again. The real problem being when it's happened to someone you love, you know it can indeed happen to anyone.

The pain of missing Mum physically hurt after a while, it felt like a massive part of my insides had been scooped out, leaving an internal hole. The strange thing about that was it came when I felt I had started to heal from the initial loss. Grief is such a lonely, and in all honesty, bizarre endeavour.

Someone told me the depth of your grief reflects the love you felt.

I often thought of something Mum used to say to

me; "Don't cry because it's gone, smile because it happened."

We can only hope that Mum has been reunited with Dad and they are sat on that bench eating chocolate, or, should I say, drinking red wine.

AT THE END OF THE

AFTERMATH

I mentioned initially that I hoped writing this book would be cathartic to me, has it been? In all honesty and in the spirit of transparency I would say no. It has been extremely difficult reliving some of the darkest hours of my life. Parts of my life I had tucked safely away in my subconscious were yanked back out and again became the forefront of my thoughts. As I ploughed through this it soon became apparent this was not for me but for others who may be going through a similar scenario. I'm hoping it will let others realise that what they feel is normal and they are not alone on this ridiculously lonely journey. Above all, if it raises awareness of this horrible horror to any women then that was my aim ... job done! This I have done for my Mum, who had a life she was so desperate and determined to keep on living. I am hopeful something positive can come out of her experiences to leave a legacy she deserved so much.

I really wish this book had a happier ending, more than anything. As sad as the end result, I hope this gives anyone else confronted with a similar battle some strength. Every single person is unique and, although there will be similarities, every person will be individual on their voyage with a unique end result.

Please. Never. Give. Up. Hope.

P.S. fuck you fucking cancer!

MUM

"Your Mum was an amazing lady, such sad news."

*

"So sorry to hear about your Mum, have such fond memories."

*

"Your Mum is a light that will never go out."

*

"Your Mum was wonderful; we are going to miss her so much."

*

"She was the most wonderful, warm, and human person. I loved her so much."

*

"Your lovely Mum, I remember her with such fond memories, how kind she was when my Mum was ill and just what a lovely lady she was, my heart is breaking for you all."

*

"I'm so, so sorry. Thinking of you all and will miss

your Mum a great deal, we are very lucky to have had Jan in our lives."

*

"Very sad news. Such a wonderful woman. I loved her."

*

"I'm totally heartbroken, she was a massive part of my childhood and I will always remember how much she did for us all."

*

"Jan was a very special lady and I feel so lucky to have known her and to cherish such wonderful memories."

*

"My Nanny loved a chat, she made me laugh all the time. I love her loads and will miss her a lot."

*

"Your Mum was inspirational and hilarious. What a lady!! Be proud."

*

"Your Mum must have been truly amazing as she created you."

*

"Your Mum is one in a million."

*

"Such a strong, independent, caring, and intelligent lady."

*

"Jan was an absolute diamond."

*

"I will miss our midnight chats on Facebook when we were both tucked up in bed. I will miss you forever, dearest Jan."

*

"Your Mum was a beautiful lady inside and out. She will now be at peace with your beloved Dad."

*

"I remember your Mum from years ago, she was always smiling."

*

"Jan was the kindest, loving, most clever person you could wish to meet, united now with her loving husband and recently departed friends."

*

"Her awesomeness will live on in you and your beautiful family."

*

"I love Nanny very much. All the memories we had are very special. I loved shopping with her. I will never forget her."

*

"Your Mum was an amazing lady, beautiful inside and out and special to so many people. If we could all have half of her strength, spirit, and determination!"

*

"Such a strong, positive lady full of love."

*

"Your Mum was my right hand. My best friend ever."

*

"Your Mum was a true friend to me. I think her fundraising party was a gift to us, friends and family, to enjoy the simple things and remember her."

*

"I miss her already."

*

"I don't know what to do without your Mum, there's a hole that will never be filled."

*

"Your Mum was so brave, so positive, so inspiring! I have never known anyone quite like Jan."

*

"You have lost a very dear person; I have lost a very dear friend."

*

"I will miss Jan, she was my dearest friend, a generous, kind, and much-loved person."

*

"Her home was always a haven of warmth and welcome, especially her kitchen which became like a second home to me back in the day."

*

"We are so sorry to have lost our lovely friend. We go back such a long way that it is almost unthinkable that she is no longer with us."

*

"Even though I hadn't known you very, very long, you were just like a Nan to me. You were so special to me. I am so blessed to have known you and I will always love you."

*

"Your Mum was the sister I never had."

*

"Thank you for all that you did and who you were for me, Nan. You will never be gone because everything we do echoes the lessons you taught and the love you gave. I won't say goodbye as you are here with me wherever I go."

*

"Jan was such a warm, spirited, and intellegent lady. From politics to her lastest craft endeavors, we always found something to have a good natter about. I will miss her very much."

*

"I could not have wished for a more inspiring Nan. The traveller, the storyteller, the Welsh cake baker. I am so lucky to be able to call this incredible women my Nan."

*

"If I look up into the sky and see two stars colliding I know it will be Nanny marrying Grandpa again in heaven. I love you Nanny and I loved it when we went to the beach with Uncle Tony and when we went to Cuba. You're the best Nanny and I loved talking to you and laughing."

*

"I love Nanny because I loved making arts and crafts and Christmas decorations. I miss you."

*

"Your Mum always spoke so proudly of you all, especially her grandchildren. A lovely warm lady and I was glad to have known her."

*

"Thank you for being one of the best role models a girl could ask for. Your strength and determinism showed me that there is nothing a person can't do if they put their mind and soul into it. Plus, that strong determinism came in very handy when you taught me to bake and sew. I love you and miss you more than words can explain but I hope that you are finally at peace."

*

"Your Mum was a superstar and no doubt one of the proudest Mums ever."

ABOUT THE AUTHOR

Sarah is a Mum of three; one son and two daughters.

A nurse of 25 years by trade, currently about to embark on a lecturing career.

Sarah is very family and friends orientated, loving all things social. Her main social love is music. Gigs and festivals consume her calendar.

Printed in Great Britain
by Amazon

55143719R00084